TENACIOUS FAITH

HOLDING ONTO JESUS

DEBORAH STEPHENS DAVIS

WestBow
P R E S S
A DIVISION OF THOMAS NELSON
& ZONDERVAN

Copyright © 2021 Deborah Stephens Davis.

All rights reserved. No part of this book may be used or reproduced by any means, graphic, electronic, or mechanical, including photocopying, recording, taping or by any information storage retrieval system without the written permission of the author except in the case of brief quotations embodied in critical articles and reviews.

This book is a work of non-fiction. Unless otherwise noted, the author and the publisher make no explicit guarantees as to the accuracy of the information contained in this book and in some cases, names of people and places have been altered to protect their privacy.

WestBow Press books may be ordered through booksellers or by contacting:

WestBow Press
A Division of Thomas Nelson & Zondervan
1663 Liberty Drive
Bloomington, IN 47403
www.westbowpress.com
844-714-3454

Because of the dynamic nature of the Internet, any web addresses or links contained in this book may have changed since publication and may no longer be valid. The views expressed in this work are solely those of the author and do not necessarily reflect the views of the publisher, and the publisher hereby disclaims any responsibility for them.

Any people depicted in stock imagery provided by Getty Images are models, and such images are being used for illustrative purposes only. Certain stock imagery © Getty Images.

Scripture taken from the New King James Version® Copyright © 1982 by Thomas Nelson. Used by permission. All rights reserved.

ISBN: 978-1-6642-5043-7 (sc)
ISBN: 978-1-6642-5044-4 (hc)
ISBN: 978-1-6642-5042-0 (e)

Library of Congress Control Number: 2021923533

Print information available on the last page.

WestBow Press rev. date: 12/9/2021

CONTENTS

CONTENTS

PREFACE

Truly my soul silently waits for God;
From Him comes my salvation.
He only is my rock and my salvation;
He is my defense;
I shall not be greatly moved.
—Psalm 62:1–2

I recently had a fantastic opportunity to speak to a group of women at an event called the Power of the Girl luncheon. This meeting is not a women's rights event, nor is it for teenagers or young twenty-somethings. It is a gathering of women in positions of leadership. This event is the result of a seed that God planted in the heart of my friend Nikki Sherrill Wyatt. The entire purpose of the meeting is for women in various leadership positions to come together, recognize God's power in their lives, and develop the ability to stand up for themselves and one another.

About six months before the event, Nikki asked me if I would be the keynote speaker. I was astonished and honored. I was also concerned because I'm not particularly eager to travel. Being held in Reidsville, North Carolina, this event is quite a distance from where I live in Temple, Texas.

This trip would require that I leave Texas on a Friday after work, speak on Saturday, and fly back Saturday evening. Trying to make the journey happen is a lot to do while keeping a work schedule. I prayed about it and, although a bit concerned but believing that God had everything under control, accepted the engagement.

Immediately, I began thinking about what God would have me to say to this group of women. After several days of pondering and praying, it was apparent that "Tenacious Faith" would be the title. I am not sure what led me to that title, but one morning, I woke up and just knew that was it. In true Deb fashion, I took time and thought about the most important concepts regarding faith until I understood what the main points would be, and then I let them roll around in my head and heart.

Three weeks before the event, while sitting in church, I had the horrifying realization that some of the women attending the luncheon might never have heard the plan of salvation. It suddenly became quite clear that if people in the audience didn't know Jesus, the whole speech would be meaningless to them. I know I should have been listening in church, but God and I had something we needed to work out. So there I sat, talking with God, and seeking a quick and transparent way to demonstrate the gospel. I would love to tell you that God dumped the whole thing right into my brain instantly. He didn't. It came to me a little piece at a time.

As soon as I got home from church, I was overwhelmed with the urgency to find my pink shawl. I am not sure where it came from, but this hot pink shawl has lived on a hanger in my closet for years. I have never worn it. It has just occupied space in my closet. Once I had located the shawl, I waited for the next piece of the puzzle.

It wasn't long before I realized that I needed a poster to demonstrate the connection between God and humans. I spent the day trying to make my own; it was a colossal fail. It is quite clear that I am not an artist. Finally, out of desperation, I went to a craft store, and would you believe they had one print of the painting *The Creation of Adam*, by Michelangelo. It was marked on clearance for $6.95. Now that I had all of the materials that God had put into my head, I had to uncover the message he had buried in my heart.

As I sat pondering and praying about which words I should use to explain the gift of salvation, an image began to develop in my head and heart of the poster cut in half and separated with the shawl stretched between them, and I knew what I was supposed to do. For those of you who have been through discipleship training, you will recognize this explanation of the gospel as a bridge between God and humankind. I truly believe that God showed me how to demonstrate the bridge memorably and in less than five minutes.

The stage was set. The halved print was displayed as if it had not been split into two sections. I stepped onto the speaking area. It was not a stage, just a space in front of the tables. I paused and looked out across the room full of women. It was a beautiful sight. There were about one hundred women in that room, ranging from teenagers to seniors. In the sea of faces, I could see a variety of races represented. I was stunned at the beauty of the picture before me. I began introducing my presentation in a standard way, telling the women I was glad to be there. I told the group we were going to talk about tenacious faith but needed to cover a little background first.

I stood next to the poster and said, "At the beginning of man's existence, man and God were close. They walked and talked together. They lived in connection with one another. One day, as the result of man's choices, sin entered the world, and a vast chasm developed between God and man." As I was speaking, I placed the part of the print with God's hand on a stand about four feet from the section with Adam's hand and continued speaking.

"God had a plan. He had a gift for humanity." I pulled out a gift box that I had painted gold and held it up. As I placed the box on the chair next to me, I said, "Some people get the gift and set it aside and say, 'I don't know what you are talking about. I never got a gift.'" Next, I picked up the box and, while shaking it, said, "Others shake the box and inspect it and say, 'I don't want this gift.'" Holding the box up, I continued, "Still others take the gift, and they are so proud of it. They show it to everyone, saying, 'I got a gift from God! Isn't it pretty? You should get one too!' But they never open the box." As I began to open the box, I continued, "Finally, there is a group of people who open the box and truly discover the gift."

I took out the shawl and stretched it across the floor between the two posters. As I walked across the strip of pink fabric between the prints, I said, "These are the people who understand the gift is Jesus, and he is God's way of bridging the gap caused by sin. They use the gift to cross over the chasm of sin to God. But then, there are those,"—I bent down and, in one motion, scooped up the shawl and wrapped myself in it—"who wrap themselves in the gift. It becomes their identity. Wherever they go, the gift is visible.

It is a part of them, and going anywhere without it is not an option."

The acceptance of the gift in its entirety is the point where tenacious faith begins. Unless you open the gift, walk across it to God, and wrap up in it, you will not have what you need to develop tenacious faith.

INTRODUCTION

Two are better than one; because they have
a good reward for their labor. For if they
fall, the one will lift up his companion:
but woe to him who is alone when he
falls; for he has no one to help him up.
Again, if two lie down together, they will
keep warm: but how can one be warm
alone? Though one may be overpowered
by another, two can withstand him. And
a threefold cord is not quickly broken.
—Ecclesiastes 4:9–12

It may come across through the pages of this book that
I have it all together. I don't. I am writing this book as a
guide. It is from one broken and failed human to another.
While I pray it will be some benefit and bring hope to my
fellow travelers, it is truly an account of what has worked
for me. If you find that some of the ideas here work for
you, please share them. I believe that this is the time for
Christians to stop bickering and band together. We are all
in the great race of life. Trust me—it will go better if we
run together, encouraging and helping one another.

As I have worked through some difficult emotions

while writing this book, it is only fair that I acknowledge the faithful support of my husband and mother. Both have been tireless in reading and helping me to revise. They have also been gracious enough to allow me to use them as examples.

In this book, you will read of many exceptional people who have had a hand in shaping who I am. Some of them have already gone on to be with the Lord. Others are still here doing the Lord's work. They are all significant in my life story. I am grateful for each of them.

ONE

THE FOUNDATION

When the whirlwind passes by,
the wicked is no more,
But the righteous has an
everlasting foundation.
—Proverbs 10:25

Have you ever been struck with one of life's events that was so painful and overwhelming that you wondered how you would survive it? During that time of pain and suffering, you may have found yourself asking some of the following questions: Where is God? Why would God allow this? How can a gracious God allow this suffering? If you did, don't worry. You had an entirely human reaction to pain and fear.

This type of response is in Luke 8:22–25. The event unfolded something like this: Jesus and his disciples had finished ministering to a large group of people, and in my imagination, Jesus said, "Hey, guys, let's get in this boat. We can take it to the other side of the lake." You know the story. They were in the middle of the Sea of Galilee when a massive storm hit. Keep in mind that storms on the Sea of

Galilee occur suddenly with no warning. This storm was so violent that the boat began taking on water within minutes, and the disciples were terrified. Four of the disciples had been fishermen and spent much of their lives on that very body of water; these guys were not overreacting. They were scared, and they wanted Jesus to do something.

Where was Jesus? He was curled up in the bow of the boat, sleeping like a baby in a rocking cradle. People, hear me on this: Jesus was not aloof to their suffering or their fear. Jesus was not just taking care of himself. The reality is that Jesus did not need to react because he knew the outcome of the journey. Because he knew what the result was going to be, the storm was irrelevant. The storm had no bearing on the outcome. So what happened? The disciples woke up Jesus and notified him they were going to die.

At this point, I want to rebuke the disciples, but I can't.

I don't know how many times I have called out to the Lord during storms of my life and said, "Jesus, wake up! Don't you see what's going on here? I'm dying!" I can tell you that it is too many to count.

But let's get back to the story. Jesus woke up and did two things. First, he rebuked the wind and the storm. Instantly the storm quieted. Second, in the calm after the storm, Jesus rebuked his disciples for their lack of faith. You see, at the beginning of this story, Jesus said that they were going to get into the boat and cross to the other side of the lake. He didn't mean they were going to get into the boat and perish along the way. Jesus rebuked the disciples for not having faith that he could get them where they were going. If they had faith, they all might have been napping through the storm.

Through trying to find how to have peace in the middle of the storms of life, I discovered the concept of tenacious faith. As I have held tightly to Jesus, sometimes only mildly complaining and other times yelling and screaming, I have found a few ways to remain steadfast during life's storms. Before we examine how to have tenacious faith, we have to determine what it is. We will look at each word separately. Let's begin with the word *faith*. Faith is that unwavering belief that cannot be validated except by placing enough trust in it to test it.

The Bible tells us in Hebrews 11:1, "Now Faith is the substance of things hoped for, the evidence of things not seen." While the words are easy to understand, the concept isn't. By looking at some examples of faith, we will be able to develop a clearer understanding of the concept. Take Noah, for instance. Here is a man who was living honestly in a dishonest world. Noah was decent enough that when God got fed up with humankind, he decided to preserve him as the new start of the human race. Let's set the stage here. Before the flood, there had never been any kind of flood. We will pretend there is no debate among Christians regarding how the environment worked before the flood. Some Christians say it had never rained before the flood, and others say that the Bible doesn't provide that information. We will start at a point at which we can agree.

God told Noah to build a giant boat in the middle of dry land, and he did. When I say giant boat, I mean *giant*. According to scripture, this boat had about as much space as 250 railroad stock cars. It held between twenty thousand and forty thousand animals the size of sheep. It is one giant boat.

Let's step back a moment and think about Noah. Here

we have a guy who was relatively nondescript. He was a tenth-generation descendant of Adam. When he was five hundred years old, he became a father. There is not a lot of additional information about Noah except that he actually walked with God. In other words, God was his friend.

When he was about 480, God's 120-year countdown to humankind's destruction began. We are not exactly sure when Noah started building. Some scholars believe he began construction on the ark before his sons were born. The Bible tells us that Noah had sons when he was five hundred years old, and the rain started to fall when he was six hundred years old. Sometime before Noah turned six hundred, he built an ark. I know that it would not be easy to gather the materials necessary to build an ark. That alone would require a sufficient amount of resolve. I am relatively confident the local lumber store does not have the amount of pitch and gopher wood Noah needed to build the ark.

Building an ark is not a small, do-it-yourself project. There is an expense; it takes a lot of resources. Along with the resources, it takes a significant amount of skill. What kinds of skills did Noah have? The Bible tells us that after the flood, Noah became a vinedresser. Most likely, he returned to his pre-ark-building employment. The skill set of a vinedresser is very different from the skill set needed to build an ark. Noah's occupation before his position as an ark builder is not recorded in scripture, but I wonder if his first woodworking craft was the ark.

I can see it now. Noah has drawn out how he thinks the ark will look. He has taken notes from God and knows what materials he is going to need. In his hand is the list of additional tools that will be required. Knowing that there is no local hardware store, he heads next door to borrow tools. He knocks on his neighbor's door; please keep in mind that he is over 480 years old. His neighbor answers the door, and Noah asks to borrow tools to build an ark.

Okay, so that probably didn't happen. Realistically, we don't know a lot about Noah, except he is a good guy who is just trying to do the right thing in a world that is not doing the right thing.

In today's world, every Christian should feel like Noah. Living in a world full of disobedience and discord, Christians should stand out like a man building a boat in the desert. I am quite sure Noah felt alienated. Surely, he was different from his peers or God would not have found him innocent and the others guilty.

It amazes me when I think of how different from society Noah must have been. I feel like it is necessary to stop here and say that Noah was not perfect. Nowhere does scripture connect Noah's righteousness to his works. What scripture says is that Noah was counted as righteous because he walked with God. Simply, Noah's relationship with God made him clean. Please keep in mind that Noah found grace in the eyes of the Lord. It all boils down to Noah's being the only man on the earth walking with God. Everyone else had abandoned God. Talk about an abundance of negative peer pressure.

So here we have Noah, living in communion with God. Then God called him out of his obscurity and told him to do something that would cause him to stand out like a sore thumb. It is quite possible that, for roughly the first five hundred years of his life, Noah managed to live under the radar. Then God told him to build a boat—a big boat.

Noah had a decision to make. He could either continue in his life of obscurity or go big.

Can you imagine what his neighbors were thinking? I am quite sure the president of his homeowners association had a problem with his building an ark in his front yard. Do you think he faced ridicule for ruining the neighborhood? At the very least, the ark became a symbol of the godlessness of the world. When God's plumb line is held up to sin, discomfort and animosity are created. I am quite sure the ark garnered criticism and most likely hate.

If we use Noah's calling as an example, why would so many Christians think following God's calling would be easy? Why are Christians surprised when others do not understand their calling? I look at Noah and am sure his friends and family thought he was a nut. At the very least, they must have believed that he was overzealous or misguided. The Bible doesn't say how people responded to him. I have to think that, in many ways, Noah felt alone in his conviction. But it doesn't matter; there he was, day after day, building a big boat. Against all the odds, he was building a big old boat and dodging insults and criticism. He had no indication that he was on the right track, but he kept building the big old boat. No one thought there was any value to what he was doing until the rain started. The best we can tell, it took somewhere between 50 and 120 years of building for Noah to complete the ark.

Let's stop for a minute and connect the story of Noah to the concept of faith. Is it possible that faith is continuing in the behavior God has called you to even if there is no indication or validation that you are on the right track? You know that Noah could have hung up his hammer and said, "God, this is too big, too hard, too expensive, too crazy."

He didn't. He just kept on building. I just wonder if, during this time, his wife shared her concerns about the well-being of the family, his pension, their insurance, or his savings account. In this whole story, her name is never provided, and she is not called righteous. Was she only saved from drowning because of her relationship with Noah?

We don't know much about how Noah's family responded to his ark building. Perhaps they helped him out. It stands to reason that one man would not be capable of creating such a massive vessel alone. The scripture does not say; for all we know, Noah's family thought he was crazy.

What kinds of craziness are you being called to accomplish? At the very least, we are called to live a very different life from the rest of the world. The good news is, unlike Noah, you are not alone in this task. The bottom line is that no matter how crazy Noah's calling sounded, he obeyed God.

Someone reading this may be thinking, *If God speaks to me, I will do what he tells me.* Please keep in mind that Noah was obedient even before God spoke to him. Obedience for Christians starts where it started for Noah—it is a life lived in communion with God. Was Noah perfect? No, he was far from perfect. Just like every great man of the Bible, except Jesus, Noah was flawed. This reality is not an excuse to live in your flaws or sins. God calls us to desire him above all things. When we do this, he comes alongside and provides the wisdom and strength for us to be obedient.

As long as we are talking about faith, we have to mention Father Abraham. Abraham is noteworthy because his faith was counted to him as righteousness. How do I know this? I know because the Bible says it in four places—really, five, but since two of them occur in Romans 4, I am counting them together: Genesis 15:6, Romans 4:3 and 22, Galatians 3:6, and James 2:23. So just what did Abraham do that demonstrated faith?

He believed that God would do what he said he would do. God promised Abraham that, although he had never produced a child and he and his wife were clearly too old to have children, he would have a child. And Abraham believed him. Now, I can tell you that although Abraham believed, he lived his faith imperfectly.

We can learn a little something from him. You see, God made the promise, and then some time passed. Sarah still had not become pregnant, so she said to Abraham, "Dear, we know that God will give you an heir, but I am entirely too old. Go ahead and sleep with Hagar, and that is where your heir will come from." Please don't condemn Sarah and Abraham for doing this; I think it is normal for us to try to "help God out" from time to time. Like Abraham, we believe that God can, but either he is taking too long or is not doing it the way we think will work. So we step in. I am going to be very honest—every time we do this, we create an issue.

God did provide a son through Hagar. That son, Ishmael, became the father of the Arabic Muslims. Eventually, Sarah and Abraham had a child and named him Isaac. Even today, the descendants of Ishmael and the descendants of Isaac are fighting over the land and lineage of Abraham. Please understand, I am not calling Ishmael a mistake. God also made a promise to Ishmael's mother, Hagar and kept it just as he kept his promise to Abraham.

Regardless of Abraham's imperfections in living out his belief that God would give him a child, God regarded

Abraham's belief as righteousness. But what does that mean? To be righteous is to be right with God. The Bible tells us that to be right with God means that we must have faith.

If we have learned anything from Noah and Abraham, faith is the key. For Noah, his faith resulted in his being safe during a flood. For Abraham, his faith made him the father of many nations. Like these two men of God, Christians should be marked by their faith. Christians must cling to an overwhelming belief that God can and will do what he says he will do. It is not an instant faith but one that bears out over time.

Again, for both of these men, faith is not instant. We know that about one hundred years ticked by from the moment Noah was notified that humankind would be washed off the face of the earth until the rain started to fall. For Abraham, it took about twenty-five years from the time God told him that he would be the father of many nations until Isaac was born.

Unfortunately, in our world of instant everything, I am not sure how many of us have the perseverance to hold on with no evidence of progress for twenty-five years. We know that faith is an unshakable belief that God can do what needs to be done to enable us to fulfill our callings. Now we need to take a look at the tenacious part of tenacious faith.

Tenacity is the refusal to let go. I suppose you can say that Noah had tenacious faith as he built the ark. Year after year, with no proof there was going to be a flood, against all of the odds, he continued building. What about Abraham? Well, he waited about twenty-five years to see the son God promised him. How hard is it to trust God year after year for a promise that seems impossible?

I am going to be very honest: personality has something to do with a person's initial ability to be tenacious. Some of us have an unwavering stubbornness from birth, and some of us must develop it. Like every other characteristic, tenacity is strengthened and honed. But how? It is established through believing and waiting for an answer. We all tend to be a lot like Abraham; if the answer doesn't come quickly, we try to help God out. It is funny how arrogant we are. We are tiny little finite creatures thinking we need to help out infinite God. Before we can develop the characteristic of tenacity, it is essential to understand what tenacity is.

I never really thought about it, but the dog given the reputation for tenacity is the English bulldog. Do you know what bulldogs are bred to do? Get ready for this. They are produced for the sole purpose of fighting bulls.

The bulldog is bred in such a way that its nose is sloped upward. This physical attribute enables the bulldog to breathe without letting go of something it has in its mouth. While I have never seen a bulldog fight a bull, I was raised in Texas, and I have been to too many rodeos to count. I know how a mad bull looks. I have seen them buck, gore cowboys, and throw a bullfighting barrel that weighs about seventy-five pounds. An angry bull is a terrifying and dangerous creature. Weighing in somewhere between 900 and 1,500 pounds and standing around five feet tall, the average bull is quite massive. Bring in the bulldog. The average bulldog stands under two feet high and weighs in at under 120 pounds. Does this look like a fair fight to you? It doesn't to me.

In the early days of bullbaiting, the sport where a dog is sent out to fight a bull, it was typical for a one-hundred-pound dog to topple and kill a bull weighing close to a ton. Are you surprised? I am both shocked and curious. The bulldog is considered tenacious because it grabs hold of something much bigger than itself and doesn't let go until it is either the victor or dead. Wow, that is a sobering thought.

For the bulldog, tenacity is grabbing ahold of something much bigger than it is and hanging on through the bucking, hanging on through the snorting, hanging on through the kicking, hanging on through the dirt and blood and slinging of snot until either the bull or the dog is dead.

When we talk about tenacious faith, it means hanging onto God's promises and God himself until the promise is fulfilled or until we die. If you think it is easy, think again. As my dad used to say, "Christianity is not for the faint of heart or sissies." Although there is no easy, cut-and-dried way to develop a tenacious faith, I have found that developing several characteristics can help. The acrostic below helps in remembering them.

Thankful
Evangelistic
Nonsubjective
Authentic
Courageous
Impervious
Obedient
Unbridled
Selfless

Here we go.

TWO

THANKFUL

In everything give thanks; for this is the
will of God in Christ Jesus for you.
—1 Thessalonians 5:18

It is a commonly held belief that the attitude of
thankfulness only occurs as a result of surroundings,
situations, or circumstances. For example, I am thankful
for the gift, help, rain, or sunshine. This assumption is
incorrect. Like many emotions, thankfulness is a choice.
It is a point of view. It is a decision. While some might
write off this view of thankfulness as just some form of
optimistic living, it isn't that. It is so much more.

Recently, I was reading a secular post on the difference
between gratitude and thankfulness. The writer asserted
that the difference is that gratefulness requires something
outside of oneself. For example, a person is grateful for
someone's help. Thankfulness, on the other hand, is a
feeling that is entirely generated as a result of choosing an
attitude. The author is half right.

This secular author advocated that all people should
be thankful rather than grateful because being grateful

demands the individual be dependent on someone else. As I write this, I smile, thinking that thankfulness and gratefulness are both choices. The catch is that they are choices that are made possible by a singular reality.

They both come from a place of recognizing God's goodness and of understanding that what I have been given is so much better than I deserve. Both are the natural and pure response to the overwhelming experience of being blessed.

Neither can truly exist without a relationship with God. Let's focus on thankfulness. It is an emotion rooted in the choice to live a life of praise and worship of the God who created and is committed to redeeming humanity. This idea is not my own; it is an idea that is made clear through scripture. Although several words in Hebrew and Greek can be translated to mean "thankfulness," we are going to look at the two that are used most often.

The most commonly used Hebrew word for "thankfulness" is *yadah*. If the word *thanks* is put into the Bible search tool, it pulls up the word *yadah*. When *yadah* is entered into the Hebrew definition tool, its various translations will be pulled up. The translation for *yadah* includes the ideas "to know," "to reach out," "to throw," "to cast down," "to give thanks," "to confess the name of God," and "to confess sin." Yikes! The translations appear to be so loosely connected that trying to understand the meaning of the word seems futile.

Stay with me here—all of these seemly disconnected definitions are connected by one concept: the act of raising hands. A person raises hands to reach out or reach up, to throw, in confession, to give thanks, and to praise. If I go through the King James Version of the Bible and look for the variations of *yadah*, the top three most commonly used meanings are "confess," used sixteen times; "give thanks," used thirty-two times; and "praise," used fifty-three times. When you look at them in context, there are clear links among confessing whom God is, giving thanks, and the act of praise. These all go together. These all result in the raising of hands in recognition of our guild and the freedom provided by a holy God.

Think about it. The knowledge of whom God is in comparison to humankind leads to an internal emotion of thankfulness, which, when expressed, comes out as praise. So much of the scripture, especially the Old Testament, elicits the emotion of thankfulness and the response of praise through describing God. An excellent example of this is 1 Chronicles 16:34: "Oh, give thanks to the Lord, for He is good! For His mercy endures forever." It wraps acknowledgment of God, thankfulness, and praise into one scripture. This scripture demonstrates the concept that when we recognize and confess God's position in our lives, the emotion of thankfulness and the action of praise come out of that.

As a side note, an unthankful person cannot truly praise God because the unthankful person cannot recognize his or her position relative to a holy God. I am sure we all have people in our lives who demonstrate this concept. It is sad. It is also nearly impossible to make people see what they have to be thankful for if their lives are not rooted in Christ.

As you know, some people, by the world's standards, have everything. They have houses, yachts, cars, beautiful clothes, and an excess of the best foods. They have every material treasure. (Now I feel the need to stop here and make it clear that having worldly possessions is not wrong or bad.) The person I am thinking of is not in emotional and spiritual chaos for what he has but for what he doesn't have. He has everything except God. For right now, this man is his own god. Because he sees every good and perfect gift as a result of his talents, intellect, and commitment, he is not thankful. He is the opposite of being thankful; he is arrogant, he is emotionally empty, and he cannot find joy in anything. Okay, so what is my point? Thankfulness is not possible without acknowledging whom we are in the presence of a holy God.

The most commonly used Greek words for "thanks" are the word *eucharisteo*, which is the verb form, and *eucharistia*, the noun form. *Eucharisteo* means to be grateful, to feel thankful, or to give thanks. *Eucharisteo* means thanks or thankfulness. Both of these come from the original word *eu*, which means prosperous and acting well.

I know that seems like a lot of rabbit chasing. The bottom line is that although the language is not as transparent as we would like it to be, there is a connection between the emotion of thankfulness and the action of being thankful. If you spend time looking at these two words, it is easy to come away with the feeling that these are not merely one-time actions but more likely a way of being.

The other thing that is very clear to me is that the words meaning "thankful" in both the Hebrew and the Greek combine the emotion that precedes the action. In the American culture, we spend a lot of time divorcing the feeling that proceeds a response from that action. For example, what are little children told about the phrase *thank you*? They are told it is what should be said when someone does something nice. They are told that *thank you* is a magic phrase to help people get more of what they want and make others like them. They are told it is the right thing to say. Children are not taught that the words *thank you* express a feeling of being blessed or given more than what is deserved. Instead, we make thankfulness nothing more than a behavior without passion.

The attitude of thankfulness is not just the one-time response of a thankful person; it is a way of thinking that continually impacts that person. Thankfulness is the understanding that something greater than oneself is responsible for all of the good that comes. This attitude creates several emotions or behaviors; the most notable is humility. Humility is not thinking less of oneself. It is thinking about oneself less. I wish I could take credit for this statement, but I cannot. This quote may be the work of Ken Blanchard or Rick Warren; it appears to be attributed to them both. No matter who said it, it is an appropriate place to start.

Our American culture teaches us some behaviors and mindsets that are antitheses to humility—things like, if you don't take care of yourself, no one will, and I have personal rights to do and say what I want. When these concepts are taught in isolation, apart from God's word, they lead to pride and arrogance without the balance of humility before God. Now, back to the attitude of thankfulness. It results in humility. Please understand that humility is not self-loathing. *Humility* is defined as recognizing one's station in the presence of a holy God. Once we grasp God's loving-kindness, we can begin to live lives of humility and express thankfulness.

One of the best examples of this type of behavior is

found in the book of Habakkuk. I have to say that, based on how the book starts, I would think Habakkuk might be an eight on the enneagram personality profile. For those not familiar with the eight, he is the challenger. Strong-willed people need things to be right or wrong, and they desperately desire the wrong to be punished. I know this because I am an eight, and the words of Habakkuk resonate with me.

This short book starts with a complaint made to God. I know we don't think it is okay to tell God what he is doing wrong, but here we have Habakkuk crying out with a complaint directed straight at God for what Habakkuk perceives as God's lack of focus and refusal to respond. For four verses, Habakkuk complains about God's lack of attentiveness to an evil issue.

Then, God answers. You would think that Habakkuk would have realized that the God of the universe answered him. But not our guy Habakkuk. He lobs additional verses of complaint against God. Then, God responds again. Throughout his answer, God asserts his sovereignty and holiness, and he concludes his response with the statement, "The Lord is in his holy temple; let all the earth keep silence before him" (Habakkuk 2:20).

That statement must have affected Habakkuk. Suddenly, having been put in his place, he recognizes the power and holiness of God. With that hurdle crossed, he takes time to build a case for the unbelievable sovereignty of God. His final words of this book have become some of the verses that I use to ground myself when trouble comes:

> Though the fig tree may not blossom, Nor
> fruit be on the vines; Though the labor of the

olive may fail, And the fields yield no food;
Though the flock may be cut off from the
fold, And there be no herd in the stalls—Yet
I will rejoice in the LORD, I will joy in the
God of my salvation. The LORD God is my
strength; He will make my feet like deer's
feet, And He will make me walk on my high
hills. (Habakkuk 3:17–19)

In short, this scripture says that although everything
looks as bad as it can get, I will praise the Lord. The
thankfulness in this scripture is represented by praising
God because of whom he is and not what he has done.
Out of the thankful heart flows praise, which is the correct
response to a holy God despite the circumstances. It is
crucial to keep in mind that thankfulness and praise are not
the response to what God has done. They are the response
to whom God is. Let's look at the final verses of Habakkuk:
"He makes my feet like the feet of a deer, and enables me
to tread on the heights." In other words, the individual
who is steadfast in thankfulness and praise will move to
high places above the chaos. This upward movement is the
blessing that comes through being constant in expressing
thankfulness as a response to whom God is.

This concept of being able to move above the chaos is
also found in Isaiah 40:31: "But those who wait on the
LORD, shall renew their strength; they shall mount up with
wings like eagles, they shall run and not be weary, they
shall walk and not faint."

Friends, this is so important. When we commit to
worship God because of whom he is, hope in Him because
of whom he is, focus on him because of whom he is, there

is a natural outcome. That natural outcome is that God lifts us, gives us strength, and helps us to climb. Here is a question. What do the deer on the top of the mountain and the eagle soaring have in common? They have a better, brighter, more expansive viewpoint. Faith in God, based on who he is, frees us. It allows us to be elevated to where we can see the whole forest and not just the tree in front of us.

That all being said, there is a sacrifice that is made for you to have a relationship with God. Don't get this wrong; it is God's sacrifice, not yours. As finite beings, we do not sacrifice anything; we only trade up in the relationship with God. Because of that understanding alone, our lives should reflect thanksgiving.

One of the best ways to express the concept of thanks to God is clarified in the words of St. Augustine, who said, "A Christian should be an alleluia from head to foot" (Catholic-link.org). King David is an excellent example of what it means to be an alleluia from head to foot, except for when he wasn't. I am just going to be brutally honest. I know from my own life that humans have difficulty in maintaining consistency. As we read about the fantastic examples of thankful people, please note that none of them were perfect in their ability to be consistent in their thankfulness. Many of them were, just like we are, moved by what they saw and experienced. They fought depression, anger, and the desire to self-medicate.

I am not saying this to give us an out for our bad behavior. I am just saying that bad behavior is a part of being human. I recently heard someone say that a detour into disobedience does not have to become a permanent path. Believe it or not, even in your sin, God still loves and wants you. His heart is turned toward you, and he is waiting for you.

Back to King David. In 2 Samuel 6:14–22, we hear of David bringing the Ark of the Covenant back to the temple. The Bible talks about David dancing before the ark. Apparently, it was quite a dance because Michal, Saul's daughter, let him have it when he arrived home. She was not impressed. In fact, the Bible tells us that she was disgusted by David, exposing himself that way. David responds how all of us should respond when accused of being too passionate about God. He simply says, "I was dancing before the Lord!" and "I am willing to look more foolish than this, even to be humiliated in my own eyes!" So, how does a thankful life look? To many, it will appear foolish and vulgar. The question then becomes, "Why should we care if we look foolish because of a passion for God?"

The reality is that the world without the Lord doesn't understand thankfulness or praise anyway. They do not have the vantage point of the eagle or the deer. There is no way for them to interpret the Christian or the Christian's outpouring of thanksgiving. So, dance, thankful Christian! Dance!

Again, I pose the question, how does a thankful life look? I think it looks like Paul, the apostle who has been called the apostle of thanksgiving. If you read his letters, you will see he is continually giving thanks for people and situations. So, let's take a look at him. Paul starts his career as an upwardly mobile young man with a job that brings him financial gain and extreme respect. He is at the top of the heap, so to speak. For those of you trying to decide what to do with your lives, Paul has a story for you. He is every Jewish mother's dream for her son and has *that* job. He is also every Jewish mother's dream for a son-in-law. Then what? He gives it up. He walks away. For what did he exchange all of these things? Well, the Bible tells us that he trades material wealth, honor, respect, and comfort to be beaten, persecuted, hated, hunted, imprisoned, shipwrecked, hungry, exhausted, abandoned, cold, and naked.

This guy who gives up everything of earthly value for a life of hardship is known as the apostle of thanksgiving. As if all of this is not enough, he also has a thorn in his flesh; we don't know what it is, but it doesn't sound pleasant. Let's not forget that along with the thorn, he has a messenger of Satan to buffet him. Yet he is remembered for his thankfulness. Really?

In 1 Thessalonians 5:18, he writes, "In everything give thanks: for this is the will of God in Christ Jesus for you." That sounds like a sweet sentiment. It is easy to say things like this when life is relatively easy and things are going well. When Paul wrote this, he had been a Christian for ten to fifteen years. He had completed his first two missionary journeys and was getting ready to start his third.

By the time Paul wrote this, he had been alienated, experienced failure, seen disappointment, and been betrayed. How can he say to give thanks in every situation? His recognition of his place in the presence of a Holy God so overshadowed everything in his life that he abandoned his comforts and safety to the service of the God, who loved and saved him.

Philippians 4:6–7 says, "Be anxious for nothing, but in everything by prayer and supplication with thanksgiving, let your requests be made known to God. And the peace of God which surpasses all comprehension will guard your hearts and your minds through Christ Jesus." Keep that thought as we get the back story of Paul.

Around AD 57, Paul was in Jerusalem, where he was beaten and arrested. While in prison, the Lord told Paul to get ready to go to Rome. Sure enough, Paul was sent to Rome. On the voyage, he was shipwrecked, and after quite a journey he arrived in Rome. During the years of his first imprisonment there, he wrote Philippians. Think about it—Paul had been shipwrecked and made a prisoner of Rome, but he was thankful.

Let's look back at the verse, "Be anxious for nothing, but in everything by prayer and supplication with thanksgiving, let your requests be made known to God. And the peace of God which surpasses all comprehension will guard your hearts and your minds through Christ Jesus." I want to point out that throughout the Bible, we are told to ask for what we need, but we are not told that God answers every prayer with a yes.

This verse is the only one I could find with a natural result for merely asking. This verse says that if you make your needs known with thanksgiving, you will be given peace to protect your heart and mind.

If you have ever been through an experience that tore your heart right out of your chest, you will understand the value of this type of peace. If you haven't experienced anything like that, you probably will, so get ready.

If we go back to the concept of thanksgiving, we must understand that the peace God provides is not related to the answer God provides. The peace that is provided is the result of the understanding of who God is. That recognition of God's sovereignty protects your heart and mind even if things do not go your way. So what does the thankful life look like? It looks like a life of complete and absolute submission to God.

I am writing something here that is not going to be popular with everyone who reads this book. When we start deciding who God is based on how we see him answer our prayers, we have removed the holiness that he deserves.

If he didn't answer all of Jesus's prayers, why would we think he would answer all of ours? The most fervent and painful prayer in all of history is found in Luke 22:42–44. The scene is something like this: Jesus and his disciples are in the garden. Jesus tells the guys to wait and pray until he returns. He goes a little way down the path.

Now the book of Luke tells us that he prayed so fervently that "his sweat became like great drops of blood falling to the ground" (Luke 22:44). Just in case you are one of those who think this is just a metaphor, there is a condition called hematidrosis in which the little blood vessels that feed the sweat glands rupture. This condition causes a person who is under extreme physical and emotional distress to sweat blood. I don't know about you, but I have experienced some days when I cried out to God passionately. However, I have never cried so fervently as to cause myself to sweat blood.

Legend tells us that even the olive trees in the garden twisted in agony at the sight of our Lord in such distress. In all this anguish, Jesus says, "Father, if it is your will, take this cup away from me" (Luke 22:42). So simple a phrase. As horrific as the next day was going to be, I do not think this prayer was about the pending pain. I think Jesus was looking ahead to the separation from his father, a separation that would occur as he would take on the sins of a fallen world. His anxiety was not about the beatings, the mocking, or the cross. His anxiety was about allowing himself to suffer the most significant pain of all, separation from God.

What is Jesus's gift to us? He has given to us what his greatest treasure is. The one thing that He values above all things is the gift of God's presence.

Let's get back to the prayer. Jesus asks God to let the cup pass. The average person, which he isn't, would become shaken as the realization of an unanswered prayer dawned. We see throughout the entire process leading to his death that Jesus is not shaken. He is steadfast in walking the path before him. He doesn't try to cut a deal, run away, or throw a fit. Everything is played out with grace and with a purpose. During the greatest unanswered prayer in the history of humankind, Jesus moves forward unshaken, unapologetic, and unwavering.

You see, he was experiencing the peace that guards the heart and mind. He had also placed his faith in whom he knows God is, not in what he thought God should do. So what does the thankful life look like? It is strength and unshakable faith in the middle of unanswered prayer.

Let's take a different look at thankfulness. Luke 17:11–19 gives us a very poignant story about Jesus and ten lepers. Here, Jesus goes to a village somewhere along the border between Samaria and Galilee on his way to Jerusalem. As he traveled along, ten men with leprosy called out to him to pity them.

Why is it important that the men had the specific disease of leprosy? Leprosy is a highly contagious disease. The symptoms include pain followed by numbness. The infected skin loses its original color, then begins to develop open sores. Ultimately, the fingers and toes start to drop off or be absorbed into the body. Due to the bunching and swelling of the skin, the face begins to take on an animalistic appearance. The smell from the rotting flesh is disgusting. Get the picture?

It is no wonder that leprosy is used to represent the destructive impact of sin. Just like sin, leprosy is debilitating, devastating, and disgusting. The effect of sin and leprosy on the individual is a slow march toward death.

And here we have ten lepers who called out to Jesus for help. You may be wondering why they did not approach him. The reason is that they were not allowed to have contact with any person. By law, lepers were required to stay away from the uncontaminated population and yell, with their raspy voices and infected throats, "Unclean! Unclean!" They were dying, and they were isolated. They yelled out, "Have pity on us!" When Jesus saw the lepers, he said something very interesting. He told them to go and show themselves to the priests. Jesus sent them straight to the priest because leprosy was considered a sin problem, and only the priest could declare them to be clean. The scripture says that as they traveled to the priest, they were healed.

I want to take a little personal diversion here and look at the number 10. I believe that God creates each situation recorded in the Bible to have a purpose, down to the smallest detail. Have you ever wondered why there were ten lepers? Would it surprise you to find out that the number 10 is considered one of the perfect numbers? It is a number that represents completion, responsibility, and the law. Think about it: the day in which the lamb was selected for Passover was the tenth day of the first month, the day of atonement is the tenth day of the seventh month, we are required to give a tenth of our earnings in a tithe, and there are ten commandments. And in this story, we have ten men who were condemned to certain death.

Nine of them headed straight to the temple—I am sure filled with excitement and obedience—to be declared clean. But one of them headed back to Jesus, fell at his feet, and worshipped. The number 9 stands for divine completeness. All of the lepers were made whole, and nine of them did what was required by the law and requested by Jesus: they went straight to the temple to be proclaimed clean. I wonder if the nine were looking for external confirmation or were just being obedient. In either case, the nine followed Jesus's instructions and were healed.

Then we have the one—the only leper who didn't follow the law and didn't obey Jesus. One is the stand-alone number, the number that shows unity and complete sacrifice for all humankind. The one man, overcome with thanksgiving and gratitude, returned to Jesus to worship.

Why do I say *thanksgiving* and *gratitude* here? This response is more than a one-time act of gratitude or thankfulness. If the man were only responding to the healing, he would have gone with the others to get permission to join the rest of the human race and, perhaps, come back to find Jesus. We do not know if the others found Jesus later and thanked him. After all, Jesus was headed to Jerusalem, where the temple and the priests were.

This one leper responded like someone who was suddenly aware of his position before God. He stood on his faith that he was healed. Unlike the others, he broke all of the rules and behaved in what could be considered an irresponsible way. He went back to Jesus and worshipped.

So what does thankfulness look like? Thankfulness looks like breaking all the rules to stand in what we know, what Jesus does for us. That one leper could have been stoned to death for his behavior, but he was rewarded instead. The other nine were healed because Jesus said they were, and the one who realized his position before a holy God was healed from more than just leprosy. He was healed from his sin.

Thankfulness is a decision. It is a choice that goes beyond everything tangible. As people, we will falter, and we will fail. We will have days like Elijah did when we pity ourselves. We will have days like Jonah did when we run away. We will have days like Peter did when we deny our Lord.

We always have the chance to come back. I have lived some pretty dark days, some I caused myself, and some that were the result of others' choices. Regardless of the experience, it is always my choice to decide to be thankful and praise God in the middle of the darkness. Eventually, like Paul, you will find that you can thank God *for* the darkness instead of *despite* it.

THREE

EVANGELISTIC

Then He said to His disciples, "The harvest
truly is plentiful, but the laborers are few.
Therefore pray the Lord of the harvest to
send out laborers into His harvest."
—Matthew 9:37–38

Early in our marriage, after a particularly tedious shopping trip to Wal-Mart, my husband looked into my eyes and, with a twinkle, said, "Do you realize you walk around like you have Jesus in a bucket and you pour him everyone?" He laughed, turned, and walked away. The funny thing about the statement is that I had never thought about it. I love Jesus, and I am going to talk about him to whomever will listen and, often, those who won't. Although this behavior fits the description of evangelism, it is only a part of what is in this chapter. It is good to understand that this chapter is not going to spend time chastising people for the way they share Jesus. We all have different personalities and different ways of sharing. The truth is that I am a talker, whether I have anything to say or not. You can count on me to open my big ol' mouth and talk.

Some people are not talkers. I have a friend who loves her children dearly yet never talks about them. Because they are so dear to her, she can't bear the thought of anyone criticizing them. Not talking about them doesn't mean that she loves them any less. Just like her, many people love Jesus but do not talk about him. A person's lack of talking about Jesus does not mean that he or she does not love him. People have a variety of reasons for keeping silent; some will be explored in this chapter. It is critical to remember that only God can look into a person's heart and know what is there.

Along with reasons people have for keeping silent, this chapter also explores why Christians should tell others about Jesus. One of the main ideas of this chapter is that evangelism is more than the words we speak; it is how we choose to live. In fact, our actions often speak louder than our words.

Although my father decided to follow Christ while I was away at college, he taught me how to follow Christ unashamedly. My father was a pseudo-renaissance type man; he did a little bit of everything. Part of his success in a variety of endeavors is my mother, but that is a discussion for another book. Let's just say he married up and go on. My dad, being the entrepreneur that he was, built some things into our family beliefs. Some of those concepts included the setting of mission, goals, and values for our family. He didn't label our beliefs and behaviors as mission, goals, and values, but they were built into how we did everything. Although, for about half of my life, my dad was what you would call a rounder, he had a strong sense of what our family was about and what we stood for.

Once he accepted Christ, the values and goals shifted, but our family's mission remained the same. It is the mission that I still use to guide my decisions and behaviors. It is my father's mission that his grandfather had given him when he was a boy and that he passed on to me. The story goes like this: I am probably about ten years old. We are at the ranch. The ranch is a somewhat rocky, mesquite-covered stretch of land in the bend of the Colorado River. It is mid-July; this is the season in Texas that is referred to as hell's front porch. It is over 100 degrees, and we are standing next to a pile of old cedar posts that need to be gathered up and taken to the dump.

For those of you who are not country people, two definitions might help in understanding this story. Cedar posts are straight pieces of cedar about four feet tall that are used to build a barbed-wire fence. The dump is a big hole in the ground on our property where we take trash and materials that we don't want.

Let's get back to the story. It is hot, and I am tired. I am quite sure that I am complaining and grumbling; it is my way. After hearing enough of my whining, my dad takes me over to a tree and sits me down. He gives me a jug of warm water and begins his story. "When I was a kid, a few years older than you, my grandfather had me out building a fence. We had worked on the fence for about an hour when my grandfather stopped to look at what we had done. He went to the end of the fence and looked back and said, 'Nope, this won't work. Bud, do you see? What you have been working on is not straight.' I looked at the fence and back at him and said, 'Granddaddy, what does it matter? The fence will hold in the cows, and it is at the back of the pasture where no one but the deer and the coyotes will ever see it. Why does it matter if it is a little crooked?' My grandfather then gave me the mission that I am passing on to you. He said, 'Bud, we have one job to do, and that is to leave this old world better than we found it. A crooked fence is not better. Anything less than your best is not better. Anyone can leave a place the same, most will leave it worse, but it takes someone special to leave it better. We are those people. It is our job. It is our calling. Just remember that.'"

With that, my dad stands up and says, "Come on, it is time to fulfill our calling." And we went and loaded up the cedar posts and took them to the dump. Some of you may be thinking, *That is a lame story.* The thing is that day established my mission.

I have spent a lifetime doing what I can to make this world better. I became a teacher to make the world better by giving children a chance. I did volunteer work to make the world better by picking up trash or helping kids have shoes for school. No matter what I do, it must make the world better.

If I am faced with doing something that does not leave this world a better place, it is not worth my time. You may be thinking that surely I do things that don't make the world better. You are correct; sometimes, I have to take time to make myself better so I can do my mission. The point is that we have to decide on some way to use the minutes of our lives. I choose to use my minutes to make the world, or my little part of it, better.

To make sure I am living my mission, I set goals to get there. Goals are short-term, sometimes daily, actions that

I plan. My work goal is to do what I need to do to improve the product or working conditions where I am employed. At home, my goal is to enrich my husband's life and make my yard and home a place where people can gather and find peace. My personal goal is to complete this book and hopefully encourage others. Once goals are set, values will guide how they are achieved.

My guiding values are summed up in one question: how I can bring honor to God as I use the creativity that he has given me, the knowledge that I have gained, and the integrity outlined in scripture to live my life? Honestly, in everything I do, I try to honor God with creativity, knowledge, and integrity. You may be wondering what all of this has to do with evangelism. Don't worry; we will get there.

I think one of the most important things people can do is to care enough about the time that God has given them to make a plan as to how to use that time. Don't get me wrong—I know that plans do not always work out. The problem is that most people just allow life to happen to them. I believe that life is too precious just to let it happen. I set out every day with at least one goal that will support my life mission. Although the plan may not work, I am doing my part to use every minute of this beautiful gift of life in a way that honors God. Life is often hard, but if we own it, make intentional choices, and use it to its fullest, it will mean something.

As I read the scripture, it is evident that Jesus had a plan for the three years of his life that he devoted to ministry. Although there is not much information about the time before his ministry started, it is clear that Jesus's life after his ministry began was well planned. You can see his goals written all through scripture as he traveled from place to place to heal people, change lives, and rock the status quo. Everything he did had a purpose, and that is to provide a visible example of who God is and how we, as Christians, should live. If we follow Christ, it is a great idea to start each day meeting with him to determine what should be accomplished during the day.

Now, my dad started each day before the sun rose. One day, as my father and I talked about God, he told me that he would get up each morning and spend time with the Lord. He said that during that time, he would pray, "Lord, if you would, please just let me walk with you today. If I can just come with you, I will help you with anything you need." As he was telling me this, he paused and, with a twinkle in his eye, added, "One of these days, we will be closer to Jesus's house than mine, and he will say, 'Bud, why don't you just come home with me.'" It wasn't too long after he told me that Dad found himself closer to Jesus's home than his.

I was living in Corpus Christi teaching school and working on my PhD when I got the call that Dad had slipped into a coma. I had talked to my parents the night before, and things seemed okay. It was a shock to hear that my father was dying. I was teaching when the page came over the speaker for me to take a call in the office.

I remember going back to my classroom and telling the students that I was sorry, but I was going home. I told them that my dad was going to heaven and I needed to say goodbye before he left. So I walked out of my class, gathered up my three children, went home, quickly packed, and drove the seven hours to the hospital. By the time I arrived, he was close to death. As we stood around my dad's bed, my mind was racing. I thought, *I will go back to Corpus Christi, get my stuff, and move back home to take care of my mother.*" I had it all figured out when my mother said, "Oh, Deborah, I don't want to forget to tell you. One of the last things your dad said to me before he fell asleep was, 'Sarah, do not let Deborah quit.'" That was it.

With one short sentence, my plans all shifted from moving home to staying the course. The next year would be the most challenging year of my life as I struggled through being a single mother, being a student, working, having financial challenges, and struggling with anger and grief. The whole time I focused on one of the greatest gifts my dad ever gave me. The gift was that one phrase, "Do not let Deborah quit." It became the beacon of light that I would focus on during the storms. It provided me with the determination to keep going.

You may be thinking that Jesus should be the beacon of light. I agree with you. I believe that God gave my dad the strength and wisdom to provide me with the one sentence that would focus my attention, stir my resolve, and keep me going. I also think that God gave my mother the power to share it with me. That all being said, they are my dad's final words; I had to live them. I had to live those words because I loved my dad and did not want to let him down. My father had told me not to quit several times during my life; the words "do not quit" did not mean as much to me until they were his last words. As he was preparing to leave this world, he was thinking about my success. It was important to him; that made it essential to me.

Jesus also said some final words before he ascended.

We call these words the Great Commission. You can find them in Matthew 28:18–20:

> And Jesus came and spoke to them, saying, "All authority has been given to Me in heaven and on earth.. Go therefore and make disciples of all the nations, baptizing them in the name of the Father and of the Son and of the Holy Spirit, teaching them to observe all things that I have commanded you; and lo, I am with you always, even to the end of the age."

This same idea is recounted in Mark 16:15: "And he said unto them, Go ye into all the world, and preach the Gospel to every creature."

Based on his words, what is the most important thing to Jesus? I know you are way ahead of me on this. Jesus's most important thought is for each of his followers to be a witness for him. Please do not get me wrong: I am not talking about hitting people over the head with the Bible, being judgmental, or walking around with signs that say, "Turn, don't burn." (It may be hard to believe, but I have seen that sign.) I really believe Jesus wasn't just asking people to take time during their weekend or holiday to go "do" missions. I believe that Jesus's last words were a request for his followers to build their life missions, goals, and values so that evangelism is not an act but a way of life. We are told in Matthew 12:34 that out of the abundance of the heart the mouth speaks. Therefore, evangelism is a lifestyle resulting from an overflowing heart. The reason for us to evangelize with our mouths and our lives is that

Jesus told us to go into the world and teach them about him.

At the beginning of the chapter, I did promise that we would cover some of the reasons people choose to keep Jesus to themselves. While there are many reasons people choose not to share the gospel, poor Jonah demonstrates one of them. He flat out does not want people to repent and be forgiven by God. The whole story is found in the Old Testament in the book of Jonah.

My shortened, paraphrased version of the story is as follows. God shows up to Jonah and says something like, "Hey friend, I want you to go to Nineveh and tell the heathens who live there about me." Jonah says, "I'd rather be swallowed by a whale." Okay, so Jonah didn't say that, but he did say no, and he did get swallowed by a big fish. While Jonah is in the fish, he has an earth-shattering thought. He decides that his current location is disgusting, and he does not want to stay in the belly of the fish. He changes his mind about going to Nineveh, and God lets the fish vomit him onto the shore. Most likely white from the acid in the fish's stomach and probably pretty stinky, Jonah goes into Nineveh and tells the heathens about God, and they repent.

The moral of the story is that, no matter how evil or sinful a person is or a group of people are, God wants them to know about him. He will go to great lengths to ensure people hear his story of grace and salvation.

It is not our job to determine if a person is worthy or not. Remember, our job is to tell, the Holy Spirit will convict, and God will sort them out.

Sometimes people choose not to share the gospel because they believe they will have to give up too much.

So let's think about it—what exactly did Jesus give up to provide an opportunity for salvation? He gave up his identity as king of heaven and became a carpenter. He gave up all of the comforts of being the infinite God and took on the cloak of finite man. He set aside his power and took on pain, condemnation, and death. None of the difficulties he faced as the Christ were a result of his sin. He chose them so we could have salvation. In comparison, when people decide to give up everything to follow Christ, it is a trade-up. Life may not be easier; in some cases, it may be more difficult. For sure, the joys are much more significant, and peace abounds.

Another reason people don't want to be evangelistic is that they believe they are not qualified. In Matthew 4:19, Jesus speaks to a group of rowdy fishermen and says, "Follow me, and I will make you fishers of men." Now I am going to tell you a secret here. These guys were not the expert anglers you see on the fishing shows, you know, the ones who are clean and articulate. Nope, not these guys. They had a small boat and a net. They had one job to do—throw the net out and pull it in. Whatever fish were swimming close by were caught. My point is that they were not "qualified" to be spokesmen for the Messiah.

But, as my dad used to say, "God does not call the qualified; he qualifies the called." Like the disciples, all you have to do is simply throw out the net you have. I know someone is wondering, *What net?* Your net is the story of what God has done in your life. If you can't think of how God has impacted you, your starting place is to get to know him first. Once you have a relationship with the Lord and spend time filling your heart with him, he will bring people into your path. All you have to do is tell them what Jesus has done for you and what he can do for them. Please hear me on this: if people who have known you for years don't know you love Jesus, something is wrong.

Earlier I wrote about my friend who doesn't talk much about her children. The reality is that everyone who knows her knows she has children because her life is devoted to them. If people know you and do not see that you are dedicated to Jesus, you have your first warning light. We build our lives around what is important to us.

Years ago, before I had a Bible app on my phone, I was sitting in an airport. My carry-on luggage was on the ground in front of me. Out of the zipper on the front of the bag, the top of my Bible was visible. A man sat down beside me and asked if I had a Bible in my suitcase. I smiled and said, "I sure do." He then proceeded to list reason after reason why I shouldn't believe in the Bible.

After about ten minutes, I gently stopped him and said, "I hear what you are saying. You need to know something. My dad died about six years ago, and you would have a better chance of making me believe he never lived than making me believe Jesus never lived." I paused, smiled, and continued. "You see, I spend my days with Jesus, I talk to him, and he talks to me. He is my friend, and he is waiting to be yours as well." Unfortunately, the man quickly picked up all of his belongings and scurried off. I think of that man occasionally and do the one thing I can—I pray for him.

Evangelism, in my understanding, is not only talking to people about God. Whether I am in a grocery store or at work and hear a need in someone's voice, I try to present Christ as the answer for filling the need. That being said, there are those people who, for whatever reason, do not want to talk about God. I am just going to be very honest with you—if someone tells me they don't want to talk about God, I do not speak with them about God. Instead, I talk to God about them.

I figure that if I can't move things in the physical world, I will work with God to move things in the spiritual realm. As much as I care, God cares more. As much as I love, God loves more. You see, Matthew 7:7–8 tells us, "Ask, and it will be given to you; seek, and you will find; knock, and it will be opened to you. For everyone who asks receives and he who seeks finds, and to him who knocks it will be opened." I believe in evangelism. There are times for us to work in the physical world, but there are also times for us to work in the spiritual realm.

Evangelism is one way we can serve God. We are not in charge. We are not in competition with other Christians. Our job is to be obedient in sharing Christ through the way we live. Being a witness for God is not difficult if you put Jesus in the bucket of your heart and keep that bucket so full that you can't help but slosh it on everyone.

I have one side note for any Christians who are choosing not to live a life in which Jesus is guiding their decisions: If you are living a life that does not reflect Christ, please do not evangelize. It is confusing. The non-Christian will not understand that you have something they don't. Please, be quiet until you have decided to let Christ work in your life. The most destructive force to evangelism is the Christian who talks about God but chooses to live like the devil.

FOUR

NONSUBJECTIVE

Trust in the Lord with all your heart and
lean not on your own understanding.
—Proverbs 3:5

As I was working on the acrostic for *tenacious*, I
struggled with finding a word that starts with the
letter N and expresses freedom from being guided
by emotions. Initially, I felt like *nonsubjective* was too
academic and dull. Honestly, it is a little stuffy sounding.
The word *nonsubjective* is most often connected to the
process of evaluation. Educators, program managers, and
managers of people all use a type of rubric or guideline to
enable them to judge performance without judging things
that don't matter.

In today's lawsuit-focused society, it is essential to
evaluate the basics of one's performance apart from his or
her personality. Judging based on a stated outcome rather
than emotion is hard to do. People naturally want to judge
everything based on their emotional responses. Whether
working in education or business, it is common to find
that managers or teachers often do not grasp the value of

using rubrics or goals to judge a student's or employee's performance.

They reject the value of the rubric not because using it is hard but because it goes against what they want to do. People prefer to judge how a project, person, or situation makes them feel. Naturally, people want to make decisions based on their gut reactions, but often these reactions are rooted not in fact but in perception. The reactions validate what the manager and teacher want to believe.

Let's face it—people are drawn to beauty and what makes them feel good. It is much easier and feels better to judge things, situations, or people based on what we think and how we feel. The problem is that our emotions lie, and the Bible cautions us against making decisions based on them.

Have you ever stopped to think about emotions? Most people probably don't think much about them; they feel them, and that is it. I find it hard to believe that emotions are simply chemical reactions in the brain resulting from a stimulus. Sometimes the stimulus is a current act or situation; other times, it is only perceived or is a memory. Sometimes the body is just chemically imbalanced, and a reaction occurs for no reason other than that.

Something I learned early on is emotions can be wrong, and they lie. For example, I have a problem with gluten. (That is an understatement.) When I consume gluten, my brain has an inappropriate chemical reaction. I am generally a happy and kind person, but after consuming gluten, I become angry, foul, and capable of saying cruel things that have no basis in any form of reality. The problem is that the thoughts and the perceptions that trigger the feelings are real to me. Even without the gluten issue, the Bible tells us that the heart is not trustworthy.

Jeremiah 17:9 says, "The heart is deceitful above all things, and desperately wicked; who can know it?" We have to understand that we are born with a sinful nature. Because of that sinful nature, everything we feel or think that is not rooted in Christ is subject to fallacy. Our best thinking and most authentic feelings will only get us deeper into trouble and further away from God.

This call to leave emotions out of determining spiritual relevance may not be popular. We live in a world where spirituality is based on how experiences make us feel. For example, we might sing a song that makes us feel particularly close to God. What if that song is not scripturally or theologically correct? Many people don't care as long as the song makes them feel close to God.

The same is true for listening to preachers. If a preacher motivates someone to feel repentant or devoted to God but the sermon or lesson is not biblically accurate, does it matter? If spirituality is just about the individual's feelings, the focus of the message is not on God.

When we focus on how we feel, we are replacing faith with feelings. It took me a while to come to the idea that my feelings and thoughts are not trustworthy and may even be destructive. Let me tell you how it happened. I have a friend named Sue. She is incredibly intelligent and has advanced degrees in Bible. For years, Sue and I have had conversations about God.

One conversation led me to believe that my thoughts and feelings are not reliable indicators of God's will for my life. I remember sitting in my car, watching my daughter do her volunteer work in the community garden.

She looked so carefree and happy, pulling weeds and watering the lettuce. I watched enthralled by her joy for living while Sue and I talked on the phone about God. I remember it so clearly. It was fall; the air was crisp. The car was off, and the windows were open; Sue's voice was full of energy and excitement. The discussion was about God existing outside of what we understand to be time and space. My mind was whirling as I thought about how God can see the beginning and end of time simultaneously, and because of this, there is no way for creation to surprise him.

At some point in the discussion, I became aware of how arrogant it is to assume I know what God wants for me. If what I believe he wants is not found in the Bible, I cannot know for sure. That day, I faced the understanding that I am not as smart as I think I am. The idea that I am born with a sinful nature that still fights to control me became real. What is even more real is that my sinful nature uses my emotions to manipulate my beliefs and behaviors. Furthermore, that sinful nature doesn't just use my feelings; it uses my experiences to help me develop thinking that leads me to a place far from God if I let it.

Going back to the word *nonsubjective*, in *Miriam-Webster's Dictionary*, this word means "not shaped by personal experience, views, opinion, or knowledge." Other sources say *nonsubjective* means to be undistorted by emotion or by personal bias. Living a nonsubjective life means not allowing what is in you—your knowledge, experiences, thoughts, and feelings—to impact your choices or direction.

Let me explain it with a story. When I was learning how to swim, I was terrified. Why wouldn't I be? I had been told my whole life to stay away from the water. I had been told that if I fell in the lake, I would drown and be separated from my family. I had also been routinely spanked for going too close to the water's edge. When the day came for me to learn to swim, my father walked to the end of the dock, jumped into the lake, and began treading water.

He then stretched out his arms toward me and yelled, "Jump!" At that moment, I had a choice to make. I could either be driven by the fear developed over time or follow my father's direction to jump. My thoughts and understanding could paralyze me, or I could follow my father's guidance and jump. I know that I hesitated, allowing fear to grip me only for a moment before I decided to jump. It was amazing. My father did just what he said he would do: he caught me and kept me afloat.

Had I leaned on my knowledge and emotions, I would have never learned to swim and would have missed out on some fantastic experiences. I would have missed snorkeling in Florida. I would have missed the opportunity to teach countless others to swim. I would have missed the joy of teaching my own children to swim. Above all, I would have missed the opportunity to rescue a child struggling to get to the side of a pool. So many amazing experiences would have been unrealized.

The concept of missing out by leaning on one's understanding seems straightforward enough, but what does scripture say? Proverbs 3:5 says, "Trust in the Lord with all your heart and lean not on your own understanding." As Christians, we are very fond of the first part of this scripture. It seems natural to trust in the Lord with all our heart, especially when the Lord is doing what we want him to do. It is not as easy to believe something that does not line up with our feelings and knowledge. I experienced this when I was learning to swim. My earthly father was asking me to do something that I knew was dangerous and scary. Trusting him was not exactly easy. Believing our heavenly Father can be even more terrifying, especially if he asks us to do something that we have been told is dangerous or risky or that we have previously failed. There have been times when I found it very difficult to trust what I believed God was telling me to do because I knew, thought, and felt something to the contrary.

When I started thinking that God wanted me to write my first book, I knew my thoughts had to be wrong! Although writing has been a big part of my job, I am not a confident writer. I have had way too many experiences that told me that writing is not my thing. When it was time for me to write this book, it was on the heels of being told that I was not a good writer by a person who should know. To say that I was a bit hesitant is an understatement.

People are funny. When we feel like God is asking us to do something easy and everything is going just like we plan, trusting God is not a problem. When it looks hard or impossible, like writing a book or revisiting a failure, we tend to lean on our own understanding. While that statement may not seem fair, it is true. Think about Simon Peter. In Luke 5:4–7, we are told that in the morning after speaking to a crowd, Jesus asked Simon Peter to push his boat into the deep and cast his net out. Keep in mind that Simon Peter was a fulltime fisherman, it was not the right time of day for catching fish, and he was tired after being out all night. His first response was to lean on what he knew.

Can you imagine what was going through Jesus's mind

as Simon Peter reacted as if to say, "Really? You want me to do what? I have been doing this all night, and the fish aren't biting." Simon Peter did not say those things, but he could have thought them. We are not told why Simon Peter relented and dropped his net into the water. I imagine that the sea began to bubble and swirl as fish jumped into the net by the thousands. Honestly, there was nothing in Simon Peter's background that would have led him to know that lowering the net again would work. His experiences, knowledge, and feelings all told him otherwise. The few seconds before he put the net back into the water, those seconds in which he thought about what he knew to be true, were when Simon Peter was focused on what he knew. That knowledge he was trusting was standing between him and a miracle. But more than that, his knowledge was standing between himself and his destiny. At the moment he stopped listening to himself and dropped the net, he found his miracle and destiny.

The second part of Proverbs 3:5 is where we are released to experience the miracle or destiny that God has planned: "… and lean not on your own understanding." The moment that Simon Peter let go of what he believed is the moment he could clearly see Jesus and what he can do. When Christians weigh whether or not they will obey based on their knowledge or feelings, their belief in God is diminished.

Let's go back to the day that I learned to swim. Had I just looked at my father and walked back up the dock to the house, I would have diminished my ability to trust him in the future. This diminished faith would have occurred because my lack of faith would be justified by my belief that walking away was what kept me safe. The reality is that my father kept me safe and opened up a new world to me. When we practice trusting without validating or judging based on our understanding, it leads to a deeper faith. When I jumped into the water and put faith in my father, my capacity to believe in him was strengthened. Like it increased my ability to trust my earthly father, obedience also leads to a more significant opportunity to follow God. The opposite is sad but true. When we feel like we have to check everything the Lord is doing by aligning it with our beliefs, feelings, and understanding, we set ourselves up for disappointment and possibly disobedience.

The next verse, verse 6, says, "In all your ways acknowledge Him, and he will make your ways straight." Many people believe that acknowledging God means giving him credit. They think that if you, God will intervene and make everything work out. Asking God to rubberstamp your idea does not always result in his intervening.

Let's go back to the beginning of the verse and add a few words to expand the meaning. Trust the Lord with all your heart (even if your world is falling apart, everything seems wrong, and your heart is broken beyond words) and lean not on your own understanding (even if you do not understand why God did not "fix" the problem or why you are feeling so lost, hurt, and abandoned). In all your ways, acknowledge him. Okay, friend, this is the hard part. This statement is not about giving God credit for the course we are on. The acknowledgment of God is so much bigger than that. It is about seeing God for who he is. God is God.

In some of my darkest days, I have been forced to come to terms with the understanding that I do not see what God sees. I do not understand what God understands. What I perceived as a perfect fix would have been utterly destructive, and what I see as chaos and failure is possibly God's perfect plan. When I acknowledge God despite where I am emotionally, physically, or spiritually, I am saying, "God, you are God, and I am not, and whatever you choose, I will do." When that is done, he makes my way straight.

Keep in mind that the Bible does not say the path will be easy or smooth. It says "straight." Remember, the road to the cross for Jesus was straight. Once on that path, there was no change. Also, that pathway led Christ uphill with a heavy load. That path resulted in a broken body and spilled blood. It was marked with a crown of thorns and mockery. When you determine that God is God and alone makes your path straight, the world may see your victory as defeat, like they saw Christ's. The reason for this is that God's ways do not make sense to a sinful world.

All of us are impacted by a sinful nature and a sinful world. You see, we are told in scripture that God's ways are not ours. In 1 Corinthians 1:27–29, we read,

> But God has chosen the foolish things of the world to put to shame the wise, and God has chosen the weak things of the world to put to shame the things which are mighty and the base things of the world and the things which are despised God has chosen, and the things which are not, to bring to nothing the things that are, that no flesh should glory in His presence.

We may never fully understand what God asks us to do, why he asks us to do it, or even how it is accomplished.

One reason we may not know is that our understanding is not essential. The only thing we need to do is to make sure we are hearing God correctly.

It has been my experience that if God is asking me to do something, I have to do two things to keep my emotions, thoughts, and experiences out of the way. First, I check to see if it lines up with the Word of God. If the request does not conflict with the Bible, I may be on the right track. The second thing I do is talk with committed, God-following Christians. I do this because these folks will do more than offer their opinion; they will fervently pray for God to guide me.

The reality is that I am required to base my decision on what I know about God and his redemptive plan. It doesn't matter if I see a way to make it happen or not. It is irrelevant whether I understand how everything is going to work out. The Christian's responsibility is to follow Christ.

So why is it important for Christians to be nonsubjective? It is because the truth is too important to be defined by feelings or human experience. If we are led only by our emotions, experiences, and knowledge, we will limit God's goodness, ability, power, and love. Truthfully, when Christians lean upon their understanding, they make themselves slaves to their intellect and emotions. The clever man surely does not have any need for God. Why should he?

The reality is that tenaciously faithful Christians must continuously call themselves back to the fact that the answer lies not in human understanding or feelings but entirely in God. Psalm 25:5 says it best: "Lead me in Your truth and teach me, For You are the God of my salvation; On You I wait all the day."

Let's go back to Simon Peter on the boat before he threw down the net. How did his understanding of the situation differ from that of Jesus? Simon Peter had very limited and limiting knowledge. Jesus, on the other hand, understood a truth for which Simon's life of experiences could not prepare him. The bottom line is that human truth limits, but God's truth abundantly increases.

The verse from Proverbs goes even further to say that humans understand the way that seems right to them, but that way leads to death. God is not messing around with this. Let me break it down a bit further. Anything that you put ahead of following God is an idol. Consider the rich young ruler we are told about in Matthew 19:16–30, Mark 10:17–31, and Luke 18:18–30. He went to Jesus and asked what to do to be saved. Jesus responded that he should keep the commandments. The young man, probably feeling smug, said, "I have done all of that since I was a boy." So Jesus added in that he should also give away all of his belongings and become a follower. The man went away. He couldn't see Jesus's truth. His understanding, thoughts, and emotions had created such a wall that he could not see what Christ had to offer. His belongings—or more importantly, the beliefs and emotions he had connected with those belongings—were what he worshipped.

How do people become masters over their desires, thoughts, and emotions so that the rich young ruler's fate is not their fate? It is the simplest yet most challenging thing a person can do. In 2 Corinthians 10:5, we are told that we must destroy arguments and every lofty opinion raised against the knowledge of God and take every thought captive to obey Christ.

I do not know what this looks like for everyone. I

know what it looks like for me. Not too long ago, I was laid off from my job. At the point in the discussion where the person letting me go asked if I had any questions, I responded, "I do not have any questions because God is in control of my life. The last time we spoke, you thanked me for my contributions. I believe if your opinion of me has changed, God has allowed it to move me to a different position."

I easily held to that reality until that night when I got into bed, and sleep did not come. Amid the tossing and turning, I was fighting with myself about what I believed about my future, place, value, and relationship with God. As each negative thought rose to the surface, I held even more tightly to Jesus. To say it was less than a battle would be a lie.

It was a painful experience that required me to stop every negative thought in my mind and meet it with what I know to be true about God and his plan for my life. Three verses served to anchor me during this difficult time. The first is 2 Corinthians 10:5. This verse tells us to destroy arguments and every lofty opinion raised against the knowledge of God and to take every thought captive to obey Christ.

During that night of personal struggle, I took every thought and argument right back to what I know to be true about my Lord. As I did that, they were put under him. Although the experience was painful and exhausting, I met the end with a peace I have never known. The second verse that held me fast is 2 Corinthians 5:7, "For we walk by faith, not by sight." When fear would try to creep in in the middle of the night, I would say these words to cut off the fearful thoughts. Finally, Hebrews 10:23 says, "Let us hold fast the confession of our hope without wavering, for he who has promised is faithful."

One of the things I found myself saying is that I am holding onto Christ. I would say it to myself, and I would say it to him. I know that the heart of Christ is gentle and bent toward those who are leaning on him. I wholeheartedly believe the scripture teaches us that we can trust the love and faithfulness of Christ and that, although he may not stop the storm, he alone can bring us through it. During difficulties, trials, and struggles, the bottom line is that tenacious faith can only exist if individuals are willing to abandon their feelings, beliefs, and thoughts for what they know to be true about God.

FIVE

AUTHENTIC

Blessed are the pure in heart,
for they shall see God.
—Matthew 5:8

A s I was thinking about authenticity, I kept returning to how critical it is to certify our identities in our world of technology. Whether it involves logging into our email, paying with a debit card, or entering a building, three common factors are used to authenticate identity. Authentication can be determined using something you know, like a password; something you have, like a security card or debit card; or something you are, like a fingerprint. Just as we apply these items to determine people's identities, we can use these three methods to assess the authenticity of faith.

Before we get started, please understand that these measures are not provided for Christians to judge other people's levels of faith. Folks, Jesus was very clear. In Matthew 7:1–6, he talked about not judging others. He said we should take care of our own areas of sin before getting into someone else's business. Grace is always the way we are to deal with others. Judgment is how we deal with ourselves.

Let's start with authentication as something you know. This authentication can be a personal identification number (PIN), a password, or the answer to an authentication question. For the Christian, authentication through something you know can be reciting the scripture, personal testimony, or statements of faith. As you look at yourself, think about what you know that points to your personal level of faith. What if I told you that this is one of the easiest methods of authentication to counterfeit? Think about it—I am sure that all of my children know the password to open my phone. They all know the PIN for my debit card and online shopping accounts, and each of them can answer the question of my mother's maiden name. None of my children are me, but they can fake it in the online world because they know what I know. Likewise, people can know all the right answers to the questions regarding faith and not be Christians. Clearly, they can be found by those who are not Christians. In fact, many atheists can answer the questions associated with faith. While this is one method used to authenticate, it cannot be used alone.

In Christianity, it is easy for people to develop knowledge without developing relationships with Christ. Many lovely people have been in church all of their lives, know all the stories about Jesus, recite the most memorable Bible verses, and point out where God is working in their lives. In case you are wondering about the last statement, God works in the lives of non-Christians as well as those of Christians. Remember that Matthew 5:45 tells us that God causes the sun to rise and the rain to fall on the just and the unjust. If God did not work in the lives of non-Christians, no one would have the desire to be saved. It is the Holy Spirit who convicts. The bottom line is that most people know what to say to show a connection to Christianity or the church.

Many people know the information in their heads but have not developed the relationship with Christ in their hearts. I know that I went to church for much of my own life, learned the verses and the stories, prayed for others, and professed to know Jesus. I was also living a life in which I was one way during the day and another way at night. I was living as two different people. I do not believe I am special. I think many people fit into this category.

When I was in college, my father sent me on a spring break mission trip. I was such a mess that the members of the mission team I was placed on threatened to quit. The short story is that by the time we drove from Brownwood, Texas, to our destination in Wyoming, I had alienated the entire mission team.

We arrived at the house where I would be staying and were greeted warmly and lovingly. I asked to go to my room and skip the meal my host had prepared. Once in the place where I would be staying the next several days, I unpacked a few things and got settled. I took out the black leather Bible my grandmother had given me as a graduation gift and tossed it onto the nightstand. I flopped onto the bed and stared at the ceiling.

I was not at all ready for what would come next. Lying on the bed angry and full of rebellion, I heard a voice. I will admit that I don't know if it was audible or not. At that moment, it was distinct enough to make me sit up and respond. The voice said, "Turn around." I replied, "No." There was a moment of silence. I broke it with the challenge, "If you can prove that I am not going to heaven, do it."

I will be candid: I don't know why I felt it necessary to challenge God. He should have squashed me right then. He didn't. The Bible fell off of the nightstand at my feet and opened to a highlighted passage, James 2:19–20: "You believe there is one God, you do well, even the demons believe and tremble before him. But will you know, vain man, that faith without works is dead?" I had no sooner finished reading the passage than the voice spoke again: "Deb, what have you done for me?"

At that moment, I felt the weight of my sinfulness. Across the page from the passage I had just read, I saw another highlighted passage, James 4:10: "Humble yourself in the sight of the Lord, and he will lift you up." I am not exaggerating when I say that I fell on my face and responded as so many before me, saying, "God, if you will just take the mess I have made of my life, I will give it to you. You can have all of it."

The change in my life was visible. That the next morning at breakfast, I noticed that everyone was just staring at me. After a few moments of uncomfortable silence, one of the guys asked, "What's up? You are totally a different person." I smiled, something I am not sure any of them had seen me do, and simply said, "God and I came to a moment of understanding and clarification last night." That was it. The mission trip went well, and that group of guys and I developed a friendship that would last through our time in college.

I want to take a minute and let you know that I have at times tried to take my life back from God. I have messed up and fallen time and time again. He is faithful. Philippians

1:6 promises that God, once he has begun a good thing in someone, will continue that work until the end of the world. To be honest, every other religion asks people to come to God and hold onto God. In Christianity, God comes to us and, through grace, holds onto us. All we have to do is accept it. Let's get back to the discussion of authentication.

The second method used for authentication is something the person has. We use a driver's license, birth certificate, debit card, and passport to authenticate people's identities. People often use their ownership of the Bible or a Bible app to demonstrate their affiliation with Christianity. Also, people frequently equate their membership with either a group or a church to being a Christian. These, too, can be forged. As easy as it is for me to get a fake ID, I can join a church or buy a Bible. These counterfeit forms of authentication can be compelling. Some people have served in churches for years and still never formed relationships with the Lord. They know about him but do not know him well enough to take a stand for him.

Just as when Jesus was walking the earth, there are different types of people who follow the Lord today. They are those who are a part of the multitude. They are following either out of curiosity or to see what they can get. We are told that the multitude of people followed Jesus when the way or road was easy and accessible.

We see in the Bible that when Jesus was about to teach something important, he went to an area that was more out of the way. Those considered the multitude fell away when the path was more difficult. The group that continued onward was the group that wanted to learn. They were more than curious but not yet committed. The second group was found on the street and in the church. These are the people who were interested in the intellectual endeavor but not in the sacrifice required to have a relationship with the Lord. They may have had Jesus as their intellectual savior, but he was not Lord of their lives.

The third group is the one we refer to as radical Christians. To be honest, they are not radical but authentic. To be a Christian, one must be willing to give up everything. I remember sitting in an adult Sunday school class shortly after the Columbine shooting occurred. The discussion revolved around the declaration of Rachel Scott, who was killed for her faith.

I remember sitting in horror as the class of twenty adults who had been raised in church voiced that they would teach their children to deny Christ if it meant they could live. I was stunned. One other member of the class joined me in saying that we would teach our children to give up everything for Christ's sake. I think the question that must be answered to determine the group we fall into is, "Am I willing to give up everything for Christ?" If the answer is not absolutely everything, you are not in the third group that follows Jesus. The third group is made up of disciples. Disciples are those who so believe in Jesus that they are willing to do what he asks. Having the appropriate credentials, though, isn't a guarantee because they, like the driver's license, can be counterfeit. Having the information and credentials must always be confirmed by the third type of identification.

Finally, the last form of identification is what you are. Fingerprints and retinal scans are good examples of methods for determining people's identities. They are virtually impossible to forge. They go to the essence of who the person is. They are not things that can be learned or picked up; they are a part of the person. For Christians, the Bible provides us with a method for determining if we are an authentic Christian. In Galatians 5:22–23, we are told that the Spirit's fruit is love, joy, peace, longsuffering, kindness, goodness, faithfulness, gentleness, and self-control. First of all, I want to reiterate that this is not for us to judge others but to judge ourselves. These characteristics are the result of the Spirit's presence in our lives. If these are not present, neither is the Spirit.

Love is the first attribute. Several words in the Greek language can be translated to mean love. The word used here is *agape*; it is the pure, sacrificial love of Christ. You will also see this word used in John 15:9, translated as "my love." The whole verse says, "As the Father loved Me, I also have loved you; abide in my love." This is a specific kind of love: the love of Christ. This is not a romantic or warm fuzzy feeling. It is an identifying type of love. It is the very foundation of a relationship that says we are one with Christ. Romans 5:5 tells us this is the love that is poured into our hearts by the Holy Spirit. Agape love cannot be experienced by those who are not Christians because it results from the Holy Spirit's work. Christian, God loves you so much that he shows this love to you and gives it to you to show it to others. Agape—pure sacrificial love—is the revelation of the heart of God. It is the element that draws the sinner into the arms of Christ. It is no wonder that this is the first descriptor of a Christian.

Agape love is so unique that it is easily identifiable. You see it in the selfless actions of committed Christians. The love that my father had received from Jesus and was committed to sharing with broken people is this kind of love. One of my fondest memories of his preaching is that he could not even say the name of Jesus without choking up. His understanding of Jesus's passion for him was so impactful that it was evident in the way he spoke. It also spilled out of him in the way he acted. Because of God's love for him, my father was able to share a sacrificial love with broken people. It did not matter what wickedness they were living; my dad was committed to loving them to Jesus. He couldn't help it. The love that draws the sinner to God cannot be counterfeited.

The second attribute is joy. This is not happiness, friends. Happiness is rooted in the temporal and is passing. This is a heavenly joy; it is rooted in the eternal and is steadfast. Paul describes the kingdom of God in Romans 14:17: "The kingdom of God is not eating and drinking but is righteousness and peace and joy in the Holy Spirit." Joy is the response to Christ's working in one's life. When a person has joy, it is clear that physical circumstances have no bearing on it.

An excellent example of this is Paul. He wrote in 2 Corinthians 7:4 that he was exceedingly joyful in all of his tribulations. In case you are wondering what kind of tribulations Paul had endured up to this point, we can find the list in 2 Corinthians 11:24–27:

> From the Jews five times I received forty stripes minus one. Three times I was beaten with rods; once I was stoned; three times I was shipwrecked; a night and a day I have been in the deep; in journeys often, in perils of waters, in perils of robbers, in perils of my own countrymen, in perils of

the Gentiles, in perils in the city, in perils in
the wilderness, in perils in the sea, in perils
among false brethren; in weariness and toil,
in sleeplessness often, in hunger and thirst,
in fastings often, in cold and nakedness.

Are you surprised that this list of experiences is what
Paul was talking about when he said he was joyful in his
tribulation? I don't know about you, but I might struggle
with finding joy in these situations. Can you imagine saying
that you find the kingdom of God in all of that pain?

Do not miss the point. That is precisely what Paul is
saying. He said that his joy was seeing God's kingdom at
work in all of his trials, tribulations, and sufferings. He
could do this because he understood that joy comes from
following God and knowing the destination is worth the
journey. I do not want to hurt anyone's feelings here, but
you and I are not the main things. Jesus, his message, his
plan, and his glory are the main things. While happiness
can be demonstrated in all types of people, only Christians
can experience joy.

Peace is the third attribute. Peace is not the absence of
chaos, but it results from trusting Jesus as Lord and Savior
during the chaos. It is more than the lack of anxiety; it is
the irrational belief that all is well during times of trial
and temptation. Honestly, it is the ability to relinquish all
care to God without looking back. While some would say
it is an irresponsible aloofness to one's problems, it is not.
It is a complete understanding of the difficulties present
in a situation and handing them over to God with the
absolute faith that he will handle it. I am sure you have
seen this demonstrated in the lives of people you know. It

is unexplainable calm in the face of lost income or financial difficulty, terminal illness, and broken dreams.

It is a genuine smile that shows a lack of fear during experiences that would cause most people to cower. It also appears as kindness in situations where most would be tempted to lash out at life's unfairness and those around them. This type of courage is rare and powerful in demonstrating the presence of peace.

The difficulty in a child's life impacts parents in ways that cannot be explained. I had the opportunity to observe the response of a woman whose child had received an initial breast cancer diagnosis. When asked about it, she said, "It was not the diagnosis that we expected. Please pray that God will provide us with the grace and wisdom to allow this experience to draw us closer to him." This response is one that can only be uttered by a person who is at peace. Her peace could only come from her faith in God, not because of what she thought he could do but because of who she knows him to be. Peace is the result of a real relationship with Christ. While others may criticize her for not asking for healing, I say her request for a closer walk with Christ demonstrates that she truly understands what is essential to God. This type of peace allows Christians to live daily in the eternal and let the temporal happen.

Longsuffering or patience is the fourth attribute. This is where many of us falter. It requires Christians to let go of the desire to judge others and situations. It is difficult, but when Christians stop judging people, their actions and motives, and their circumstances, the result is patience. Have you ever thought that patience provides the opportunity for mercy? The problem is that longsuffering is more than refusing to judge; it is about persistence in refusing to judge. It is the will to continue to reserve judgment regardless of the outcome. It means never giving up on the idea that someone can change. The word used for patience and longsuffering in Galatians 5 is the same word used in 1 Peter 3:30. This is a word used to describe God's patience as he waited for the ark to be built. It is God's choosing to reserve judgment while constantly suffering the insults of humankind as he waited for Noah to achieve the near impossible. People, it was a hundred or more years of waiting.

We live in an instant society. We are geared to believe that everything must happen immediately. This is not how God operates. The fourth attribute of peace or longsuffering always means a persevering refusal to judge another person. Longsuffering, because of the persistence required and the rejection of judging, is not an attribute that can be faked. To persist in refusing to judge another's actions or motives during times of pain or insult can only be the result of God's involvement.

The word *kindness* is the fifth attribute described in this passage. This word is used to describe how God deals with people. In Romans 11:22, we are told that God's kindness allows Gentiles to be saved. In other words, kindness is the mercy of God. You see, mercy is given when we do not get the punishment we have earned. As God shows mercy, we as Christians are called to show mercy.

Remember the story of the unforgiving servant in Matthew 18:23–35? Jesus told this story, and he prefaced it with the statement that this is what the kingdom of God is like. Because he said this, we can assume that God is the king and the servants are the Christians. It came time for the king to make sure all of his accounts were settled, so he called in one of his servants who owed a bunch of money. The king said, "Boy, it's time to pay up." The servant begged for more time to pay the debt. The king was moved by pity for the servant and forgave the entire debt. This debt was so large the servant could never pay it back anyway. I have heard the amount estimated to be two hundred thousand years' worth of debt. I don't know if that was the case, but it is a huge amount.

Feeling pretty good about being debt-free, the servant found the guy who owed him some money. It was a minimal debt, but instead of forgiving this tiny little debt, he had that guy thrown into debtors' prison.

The king heard about the evil behavior of the servant. He called the servant in and said, "Because you did not forgive, I will not forgive you." He had the servant taken away and tortured until the debt was paid. Please understand that the torture would last forever because the debt could not be paid.

Mercy is what God gives to us. He requires that, once we accept his forgiveness and mercy, we extend it to others. There are no other options. Mercy can result only from the changes the Holy Spirit makes in the hearts of Christians.

Some people think that Christians' living lives defined by mercy equals being too soft or being taken advantage of; they are wrong. Mercy is foundational to Christians' relationship with God. You may be thinking that I don't understand what others have put you through or what harm they have caused in your life. Before we look at what others have done to you, let's look at what you have done to God.

You are God's creation, made for a relationship only with him. Before you accepted him as Lord and Savior, you were an adulterer. You had relationships with others besides him; you mocked him, ignored him, rejected his gifts and affections, turned against him, and lied to and about him. Even after accepting his love, there are times you have put others, situations, or possessions ahead of him. Friend, there is nothing that anyone has done to you that you have not done to God. Because he forgave us before we knew we needed forgiveness, we are to forgive. Because he continues to show us mercy for a debt we could never pay, we are to show mercy. Mercy is one of the hallmarks of the Christian life. It cannot be falsely created.

Goodness, although it sounds like kindness, is very different. Kindness is the offering of mercy, but goodness is the offering of grace. While mercy is withholding a deserved punishment, grace is giving a gift that is not earned. The scripture is clear that, while we were still sinners, Jesus gave his life that we might be reconciled with God. His gift of eternal life and reconciliation is a gift that we are not worthy of, and it is one that we cannot repay. Christians can never out-give God, but a God-inspired generosity of grace should mark the Christian life. Think of the story of the Good Samaritan in Luke 10:30–37. A man who was on his way from Jerusalem to Jericho was attacked by a group of thieves who robbed, beat, and left him to die on the roadside. First, a priest came by, but he passed on the other side of the road. Second, a Levite, teacher of the law, came by. He also passed on the other side of the road. Third, a Samaritan came down the road. He stopped, offered first aid, loaded the guy on his donkey, took him to a hotel, paid his bills, and left additional money to take care of him.

Had the traveler done anything to make him worthy of the generosity of the Samaritan? He had not. Let me point out that the priest and the Levite were card-carrying religious people. They, however, did not demonstrate a life marked by God. Only the Samaritan, the man considered to be unclean, demonstrated a life characterized by grace. Goodness is extravagant grace that results from God's lavish gift of his son. It cannot be faked.

The sixth attribute is faithfulness. But just what is faithfulness? We studied the word *faith* in chapter 1 and found it is an unwavering belief that cannot be validated except by placing enough trust in it to test it.

So, if that is the case, what is faithfulness? It stands to reason that it is being full of an unsubstantiated, unwavering belief that is continually being validated through testing. Clearly, this is not a one-time action but a continuous action. For one to be faithful, the action must be repeated over and over again without hesitation. Faithfulness produces steadfast behaviors that can be expected and trusted. In short, faithfulness is a consistency of behaviors. While it is true that God is always faithful to do what he says he will do, it is essential to understand that the Christian life is also marked by faithfulness. For Christians, faithfulness is living in a way that is rooted in faith. As Hebrews 11:1 tells us, it is living rooted in the substance of things hoped for, the evidence of things not seen. Faith is living so that all our decisions are made based on the belief that God will do what he says he will do. For example, a faithful life pressed by injustice or violence responds with mercy and grace because Romans 12:19 says that we should not avenge ourselves because it is written that God says, "Vengeance is mine, I will repay." A faithful life pressed by physical need responds with joy because, as the scripture tells us, all of our needs are met through

Christ. A faithful life impacted by injury at the hands of others is marked by forgiveness because we are told that, as Christ has forgiven us, we should forgive others. A faithful life is one lived in response and alignment with God's Word. It doesn't matter what the situation is; the response is always in alignment with the Word.

In Acts 7:54–60, the scripture recounts the stoning of Stephen. An unfaithful person would have hurled insults and perhaps stones, but the faithful person responded with, "Lord, do not charge them with this sin" (Acts 7:60). The faithful person responded in forgiveness. At the very core of God, we see forgiveness, grace, mercy, love, peace, and joy. The faithful life is one that can be counted on to respond consistently in all of these.

While faithfulness speaks to the consistency with which a person responds, the last two attributes return to a reflection on behaviors. The seventh attribute is gentleness, also translated as "meekness." This is one of those words we see in other places in the scripture. The most notable is perhaps in the Sermon on the Mount, where Jesus says, "Blessed are the meek, for they shall inherit the earth" (Matthew 5:5). When we talk about being meek or gentle, we are not talking about being a wimpy, milquetoast kind of person. Not at all.

The word used in the Greek language for "meek" or "gentle" is the word used to mean "trainable." Follow me here. It is a special kind of trainable. It is the word used referring to training horses for war. Consider this: a horse that is trained for ground war is trained to be so sensitive to the rider's touch that it can completely override its natural responses of fear to be obedient.

Horses are terrified of blood. My dad used to tell a

story about being on his horse in the far pasture at the ranch. Way back in the trees, he saw a huge buck. He dismounted his horse, steadied his gun, and shot the deer. So far, so good. While the horse did not like the gunshot, he was not terrified. What came next is a matter of fact for country people.

My dad field dressed the deer and attempted to tie the carcass of the deer behind his saddle. This is the point when everything fell apart. A horse's natural response to the smell of blood is to run. Let's just say that my dad had a long walk back to the barn.

The Roman horse trained for battle would enter the battlefield, which was full of noises, chaos, and blood, and be wholly submitted to the soldier's touch. If meekness is being trainable to overcome natural responses to threats and fear, it is not a weakness but a sign of strength.

For the Christian, a life marked by meekness is a life that is so submissive to the will of God that all human responses are overcome. But gentleness and meekness go beyond trainability to expression. The Bible is clear that it is God who has the authority to respond in wrath and anger. Christians should respond in love with gentleness. Again, wrath may be the natural response to injustice, but being meek means that the natural response will be overridden.

People seldom hear past the tone of voice to the words underneath. Responding in gentleness ensures the message is transmitted. While using a quiet tone is not relegated only to Christians, the ability to respond to the Holy Spirit's slight nudging is something that only a Christian can do.

The eighth and final attribute of the Christian is self-control. Unfortunately, the Christian church of today does not demonstrate this. In my own life, I have done a terrible job of living a life of self-control.

So many things are out of control that I have a hard time even keeping track of them. So let's start with the basics: what you watch and listen to form your thoughts. Your thoughts will become the basis of your words. Your words will ultimately guide your actions, and the compilation of all of your actions is your character.

Christian, the first step is to be very careful with what you allow yourself to take in. Whether it's music, movies, books, or discussions, you must be selective. The easiest place to start is guarding what goes into the mind. Once inside the mind, bad ideas and sinful concepts take root as thoughts. Philippians 4:8 is very clear. It tells us that we can control our thoughts, and it is our responsibility to do so.

We should think only about things that are true, noble, right, pure, lovely, admirable, excellent, or praiseworthy. Folks, if our thoughts are not these things, we must change them. The reality is that self-control is so much easier if the mind is guarded. Stopping actions that are borne out of thoughts and words is so much more difficult.

A life of self-control is not even celebrated in our world. Very few people admire restraint because the world has told us that self-control is fearful living. Only a Christian would even want to demonstrate self-control. That is good because only a life rooted in Christ is capable of self-control.

If you are a Christian whose life is demonstrating a lack of self-control, you have another option. Come home. Like the prodigal son in Luke 15:11–32, you can come back. God is waiting for you. Just come home, repent, and start over.

These attributes described as fruits of the Spirit go straight to the composition of a Christian. These represent Christian DNA. With this all being said, authenticity has one more facet that we need to discuss.

To be authentic is to be pure of heart. It means one's beliefs, motives, and behaviors are in alignment. Jesus talks about this in Matthew 5:8: "Blessed are the pure in heart, for they shall see God." Some people will tell you that those who are pure in heart have been washed clean by the blood of Jesus, and I agree with that. *Pure of heart* means there has been a purification of one's heart that results in new life. Those who are pure of heart cannot fake that purity.

But what is the result of being purified? The result is that these individuals will see God. Although this does mean ultimate salvation, I believe it also means seeing God in the here and now. Just as the Israelites saw God leading them through the wilderness as a pillar of cloud by day and a pillar of fire by night, the pure of heart will see God's leadership in their lives. Just as Moses met with God regularly to know what needed to be done, the pure of heart will receive God's direction on how to live and serve. The pure in heart can see God and his revealed plan. Being an authentic Christian is just being a Christian. It is not about what others see in you. It is all about what you see in yourself. Above all, it is about your relationship with Christ.

SIX

COURAGEOUS

Have I not commanded you? Be strong
and of good courage; do not be afraid,
nor be dismayed, for the LORD your
God is with you wherever you go.
—Joshua 1:9

When I think of courage, my first thought is of the men and women who serve in the armed forces and as firefighters and police officers. These people make it their life's mission to charge into dangerous situations with little or no thought for their safety.

They indeed risk everything for others or their mission. So are these fantastic people without fear? I don't think so. I believe they have faith in their training, leaders, partners, and equipment that enables them to do what most of us either couldn't or wouldn't. Courage is not the absence of fear but an abundance of faith that makes fear irrelevant. In story after story in the Bible, average individuals summon courage to achieve unbelievable things. How do they do it?

We are going to look at several people who demonstrate exceptional courage as they face life's challenges.

Just a little background information first—the first five books of the Bible are called the Pentateuch, and according to tradition, they were written by Moses. These include Genesis, Exodus, Leviticus, Numbers, and Deuteronomy. While I understand that the end of Deuteronomy recounts Moses's death so clearly, he could not have written it; it is agreed that Moses probably had someone else finish the book for him.

First, let's look at Joshua. His journey to leadership begins in Deuteronomy 31. Moses had served as the Israelites' leader, but the time had come for him to hand over leadership to Joshua. In this solemn exchange of power, Moses addressed the Israelites, saying essentially, "Y'all don't be afraid; God will deliver all of your enemies into your hands." Then he turned to Joshua and said, basically, "Hey kid, you will be the one to lead these people into the promised land. Be strong and courageous because the Lord God is with you. He will not fail or leave you. Because he is with you, do not be afraid" (see Deuteronomy 31:1–8). What a handoff! No pressure here. Only the most exceptional leader known to humankind was handing off the command to Joshua.

After Moses died, the Lord appeared to Joshua and spoke to him. He explained that everything would be okay and, in the explanation, said, "Have not I commanded you? Be strong and courageous; don't be afraid, and do not be dismayed: for the LORD your God is with you wherever you go" (Joshua 1:9). I want to point out that it is not a good idea to ignore it when the Lord commands something. Why do you think God would command Joshua to be strong and courageous? Could it be because what lay ahead of him was scary?

If Joshua was told to be courageous, do you think there were other options? There were at least two. Joshua could move into his leadership in courage or in fear. God was just letting him know which was the better option. I believe this is true for all of us. When faced with the task before us, we can move forward in faith or be paralyzed by fear. We can be confident or questioning.

You see, God knew what lay ahead on Joshua's journey. He had already seen every obstacle and opposition. Nothing in Joshua's life was a surprise to God. Therefore, if God already knew and had made provision, why would Joshua be afraid? The answer that was true for Joshua is right for all of us. Joshua was afraid only if he didn't trust God to have everything under control.

One of Joshua's most notable events is the battle of Jericho. You can read about it in Joshua 5:13–6:27. Now, the city of Jericho had one massive wall that encircled it; because of this, it would be tough to infiltrate. The abbreviated version of the story found in Joshua 6:1–20 is that God told Joshua, "You need to get seven priests to carry ram horns in front of the ark of the covenant. All of the armed men will follow them. For six days, the entire group with the priests leading will march around the city one time. On the seventh day, you will march around the city seven times, blowing the trumpets. In the end, have the priests give a long blast on the trumpets followed by all of the men cheering, and the wall will fall." What a plan. Honestly, this plan sounds crazy! I don't know how Joshua felt about it, but I would not be excited about standing before my army and presenting this nonviolent battle plan.

You know how the story ends—they marched, blew, and yelled, and the wall fell. Ta-da! It all worked out in the end, but it is the middle that perplexes me. I can't help but think that Joshua might have been anxious about presenting this plan of attack. I also think there might have been some mounting concern as he and his army walked around Jericho day after day. As I think about this, it is clear that neither Joshua nor his army had any guarantee that the plan would work until they had completed all of the steps. How crazy does it sound to take basically a week to march around a well-fortified city and just expect that at the end, without any fighting, the city would be given over to you? I certainly don't know what Joshua was thinking through all of this, but I know God told Moses to tell Joshua to be courageous, and God himself told Joshua to be courageous. I just happen to believe that he was afraid but that his faith exceeded his fear. When faith exceeds fear, God can use ordinary men to do extraordinary things. Let's look at another man of courage.

Let's talk about David, the king who brought the Ark of the Covenant into Jerusalem. Because he was interested in the Ark of the Covenant, we can assume that he was familiar with Moses's writings. He had been taught about Joshua and had a history of understanding God's call to courageous living. For David, the call to courageous life was one he accepted as a part of adopted behaviors.

You may not be aware that David was anointed to be king by the prophet Samuel sometime before he went out to the battlefield to take his brother lunch and ultimately face off with Goliath. Think about this: 1 Samuel 16:13 tells us that Samuel took the horn of oil and anointed David to be the next king. At that moment, the spirit of the Lord descended on David and remained with him from that day forward. Indeed, Davis was a man with a slight edge. Folks, his courage came from understanding God's character and the fact that he knew God was with him!

Let's think about this. David knew without a doubt that he was going to be king. The prophet had anointed him, and he believed the prophet. His father asked him to take food to his brothers, who were out on the battlefield. While he was there, he heard Goliath taunting and tormenting the Israeli army. He also heard Goliath making fun of God. David had some information that no one else had—he knew what his future held. Because he knew what was coming, he also knew where his success would be. In David's mind, there was no chance that he would not be successful against Goliath. Keep in mind that no one else understood David's courage. They just did not get it.

According to 1 Samuel 17:17–51, David arrived on the battlefield and saw what was going on. He had no choice but to act. He approached Goliath and said something like, "All right, big guy, you have your weapons, but I am going to whip you in the name of the Lord. God is going to give you to me, and I am going to take your head." And it happened just like David said. Was he courageous? Yes, he was. Where did his courage come from? It was rooted in his faith in God to deliver him so he could fulfill the prophet's anointing. Courage is borne out of a knowledge that God can and will preserve us to achieve his mission. Before you think you do not have access to this type of courage, let me assure you that God has a purpose for you.

Now, most of us are not anointed by a prophet and given our future. But when we accept Christ, the Lord indwells us and gives us knowledge and strength to follow him. I will say that God's plan is always accomplished, but the follower is not always spared. Think about the apostle Steven, who was stoned to death. He was not saved from death. Without his sacrifice, Saul might not have given his life to Christ. We do not know God's ultimate plans, but I believe he provides courage for us to move forward and be a bold witness to his glory. Sometimes courage is found in the individual, but sometimes it is displayed in a group.

Three men who beautifully demonstrated courage regardless of the situation's outcome were Shadrach, Meshach, and Abed-nego. Their full story is recorded in Daniel 3:8–25. It might not surprise you to know that these three guys were friends of Daniel, the guy who was eventually thrown into the lions' den. They lived during the reign of King Nebuchadnezzar; he was an evil guy most of the time. He was a little egocentric and had a golden image created that was about ninety feet tall and nine feet wide. The Bible doesn't describe the image other than giving its size and saying that it is golden. I like to imagine it is a giant statue of Nebuchadnezzar himself. Basically, by setting up the golden image, he declared that he would reign eternally and that God was with him alone. He then made a decree that, whenever music played, everyone had to stop what they were doing and worship the golden image. He went on to say that those who refused would be thrown into a giant fiery furnace. Fast-forward: Daniel's three friends would not bow down. They absolutely refused to worship the image. To get the guys to change their position and worship him, King Nebuchadnezzar said, essentially, "Okay, guys, I am going to have you thrown into the fire. By the way, you think god is with you and I know he is only with me. Who is the god that is supposed to deliver you?" Shadrach,

Meshach, and Abed-Nego answered, "No problem about the fire, and we are not going to answer your question. The God we serve can and will deliver us. But, even if he doesn't, we will still not serve you or worship your gods." *Wow!*

They sure told the king! It took courage to stand up to certain death. Their courage was rooted in their commitment to God. It did not matter to them how God would respond. They were acting out of conviction. The rest of the story is that God did appear in the furnace with them and kept them from burning. Courage is not the lack of fear but the abundance of faith.

So far, we have seen courage rooted in God's command, courage resulting from God's call on one's life, and courage based on a commitment to God. Now, we are going to look at courage arising from a relationship with Christ. More specifically, we will take a few minutes to examine how a man named Ananias demonstrated personal courage. The full story is found in Acts 9:1–19. The abbreviated version goes something like this. Saul was an extreme persecutor of Christians. He was wholly devoted to annihilating anyone who was preaching that Jesus is the Christ. After Stephen was killed, Saul sought permission from the synagogue leaders to travel to Damascus to capture and bring back those who were preaching about Jesus. While he was traveling on the road to Damascus, Jesus showed up as a bright light and knocked him off his donkey. As Saul was sitting in the dirt blinded by the light, Jesus asked, "Why are you persecuting me?" Saul, confused, uttered, "Who are you?" Jesus introduced himself as the Christ and instructed Paul to go into town, where he would be told what to do.

Meanwhile, in Damascus was a guy named Ananias. He was minding his own business when he had a vision in which the Lord told him to find Saul and heal him of his blindness. Ananias knew precisely who Saul was. The scripture tells us that he was aware that Jerusalem had given Saul the power to arrest and return to Jerusalem with anyone preaching about Christ. He knew that he would be putting his own life in danger and endangering all of the disciples if he healed Saul. It would be a difficult spot. God was asking him to heal and take care of his enemy. Certainly, his friends and the other followers of Christ could see this as a treasonous act. Ananias, secure in his relationship with the Lord, found Saul, healed him, fed him, and took him to spend time with the other disciples. His courage, rooted in relationship and fellowship with the Lord, allowed him to put his own life and others' lives in danger. You have to understand that his courage also produced grace. The people Saul had been killing were friends of Ananias and the other Christian. Paul had been hunting them. The courage of Ananias provided a way for God's grace to be demonstrated through the way he ministered to Saul.

These are just a few stories of courage. Courage rooted in a command from God is something we all have. The scripture tells us over and over to be courageous and not fear because our God is faithful. When we truly understand who God is, it is much easier to stand in courage. Joshua could move forward in courage with what might have seemed to be a crazy plan to capture Jericho because he had heard from God to be courageous. Joshua could have quit on the sixth time marching around the city because he did not see any change, but he didn't. His courage kept him following God's instructions. Like courage moved Joshua forward, God will use your courage to keep you going. Bruce Wilkinson wrote a book called *The Dream Giver* that details the courage it takes for a nobody to achieve something for God.

Every dream given by God comes complete with naysayers, realists, and obstacles. God has not stopped giving his people crazy plans to achieve his purpose. One way to stay courageous is to keep the scriptures calling us to be courageous on our hearts and in our minds. A list of such scriptures is in the index of this book. Courage borne out of God's call on one's life comes from the understanding that we are all instructed to be witnesses for the Lord.

While the Bible teaches us to obey those who have authority over us, we are also instructed to follow the movement of the Holy Spirit. God will give you the courage to minister to people at work or to move on. He will work in you to accomplish his will if you allow him. As David had the Spirit of the Lord on him, we have the Spirit of the Lord as well. It is the Holy Spirit that leads us to minister to those around us. I have a friend named Todd who follows the Lord and seems to call when I need encouragement the most. We have been encouraging each other for over seven years. Now all I need is to hear Todd's "hello," and I am inspired because I know what to expect from him. When we first met, Todd was a new hire where I was working. He dared to tell me that he was a believer. That courage allowed God to build a friendship between us that has been used to glorify God repeatedly and lead others to stronger faith.

Courage is rooted in commitment. We can muster courage when we are genuinely committed, heart and soul.

If you lack courage in anything, look at your commitment to God. Folks, this type of courage is not surface courage. This courage is deep-rooted, "I will not be moved" kind of courage. This is the type of courage that can stand against what all of one's knowledge and senses are saying is true. This is the courage that says, "I believe God will, but even if he doesn't, I will not be moved." It is a gritty, tough, irrational, and intractable stubbornness not to be moved, manipulated, or changed. It is the courage that protects believers against their weaknesses and the criticism of others. It is rough, raw, and real. It is the courage that looks at the reality of a situation and says, "This seems impossible. Let's do it!"

I have a friend who is fighting leukemia. He is not someone I necessarily think of as being a courageous person. He is kind. He is loving. He is gentle. But there he is diagnosed with very advanced cancer. Through his three-year battle, including chemotherapy and losing all of his teeth, I have read and continue to read his Facebook posts. He posted about the reality of his disease and the greatness of the God he serves.

I watch him as he quietly, with dignity and praise, worshipped God and said, "I know that God can heal me, but even if he doesn't, I will praise him." My friend is committed to God at such a high level that nothing in the world or beyond it can cause him to falter. This unwavering belief in God, in the middle of pain and reality, is courage.

Then there is the courage that comes out of a relationship. As a teacher, I know that I can leverage my relationship with my students to help them achieve more than they believe possible. I know that their desire to make me proud and make me happy will fuel their courage to try harder and risk more. What they don't know is that I am there to keep them from failing. I hold the cards and can create a path for their success if they will just take it.

Just as God created a way for Ananias to meet Saul and successfully set up a ministry that would quite literally change the world, God makes a way for us. God, through his relationship with us, asks us to have the courage and then follow through. If we trust him, we know that he has everything under control. Like I work with my students, God is waiting for us to step out. Once we do, he will keep working on our behalf. Failure will occur only when one of us quits. God promises that he will not stop until he has perfected each of us. That means failure occurs only when the Christian quits.

My sister used to run cross-country track. When she started running track, she was not the best runner, the fastest runner, or the most competitive runner. She was a runner. She changed when my dad started going to her track meets. It was clear that she was not running for the medal or the accolades; she was running to see my dad smile and to hear him cheer.

Because of her desire to please my dad, she developed visible courage that propelled her to continue to run in all conditions—while throwing up, while injured, and while in great pain. The way she pushed everything aside to make my dad happy was indeed an act of courage. You see, she never just ran for the win. She was running for that relationship. Winning was a byproduct. Breaking records was a byproduct. Her courage came from pressing forward to make our dad smile.

I have to stop and get honest with myself here. Some of the things I am doing may look foolish, could be impossible, and appear irrational. Spending time writing a book that I have no guarantee will be published, creating a website that might never become anything, and writing a blog that others may never read all come with the fear of failure. The failure will be very public. I have no guarantees of anything. But I do know one thing: I believe God has given me this task, and regardless of my fear, I must move forward. Like my sister, I, too, am running a race. I am running to make my heavenly Father smile.

SEVEN

IMPERVIOUS

> Blessed is the man Who walks not in
> the counsel of the ungodly, Nor stands
> in the path of sinners, Nor sits in the
> seat of the scornful; But his delight is
> in the law of the LORD, And in His law
> he meditates day and night. He shall
> be like a tree Planted by the rivers of
> water, That brings forth its fruit in its
> season, Whose leaf also shall not wither;
> And whatever he does shall prosper.
> —Psalm 1:1–3

In the first century, it was common for the Jewish purification jars to be made of stone. Each jar was carved from a single stone and held twenty to thirty gallons of water. The stone jars were desired over vessels made of pottery which were porous and fragile and therefore easily made impure. Once a purification jar was impure, it was no longer useful to the owner and had to be discarded. Stone, on the other hand, was regarded as a material that could never become ritually impure. Stone was difficult to stain or break, and it was also much less porous than pottery. Stone was considered to be impervious to impurity.

Impervious is the next characteristic to be developed in the quest for tenacious faith. It means "not affected by or penetrated by anything." Christians are called to be impervious. It is true. We are to be resistant to stain and impurity just like the purification pots made of stone. We are not to be changed, stained, or impacted by the elements outside of us because we are to be set aside for the Lord. Romans 12:2 tells us that we are not to let anything in the world change us, nor should we change ourselves to be like the world. Like the purification jars, once we are saved through a relationship with Christ, we are set aside for holiness. Intentionally allowing the sinful thoughts and concepts approved by the world into our hearts and minds is equal to intentionally defiling a purification jar. Keep in mind that the purification jar, once defiled, is no longer usable. But unlike the purification jar, through Christ, we can be made clean again.

One way to become impervious is to be cautious about with whom we spend time and from whom we seek counsel. My grandmother used to say, "If you sleep with dogs, you will end up with fleas." In other words, it is expected that you will become like those you hang around. Their values will become your values, and their behaviors will be yours as well. I recently heard a well-meaning radio pastor encourage his audience to spend time not only with Christians but also with non-Christians where they hang out. Although I understand that he was basing this on the concept that Jesus hung out with sinners, I also know that Jesus had a better understanding of his calling and the human condition than any of us. While I do believe that it is important to come alongside non-Christians to share the gospel steadfastly, I also know that it has to be done with the mindset of bringing the lost to Christ. The Bible talks about with whom and how the followers of God should spend their time. Psalm 1:1–3 says, "Blessed is the man Who walks not in the counsel of the ungodly, Nor stands in the path of sinners, Nor sits in the seat of the scornful...." Even though that is not where the verse ends, let's take a minute to examine what this part of the scripture says. First of all, the word *blessed* can be translated as "happy" or "joyful." It can also be translated as "congratulations to." Whichever translation of the word you choose, you can see that the person who is in alignment with this scripture has something to celebrate.

The first type of person celebrated is one who does not make decisions based on the advice of the ungodly. So just who are the ungodly? They are those who have sinned against God and humans and live in a way that is hostile to God. In other words, the ungodly are those who choose a lifestyle that is openly against what scripture requires. Before we get too judgmental here, let's remember that Proverbs 6:16–19 tells us that seven things are an abomination to God: arrogance, a lying tongue, hands that shed innocent blood, a heart that makes wicked plans, feet that run to evil, a false witness, and one who stirs up strife among people. The ungodly live some, if not all, of the attributes. Did you ever stop to think that a little white lie is something that God considers an abomination? What about turning people against one another? These may be things we don't consider as being ungodly, but they are.

What happens when a Christian asks an ungodly person for advice? The ungodly person will give his or her opinion, and it will not line up with the scripture. For example, I was sitting in the airport and overheard a precious teenager asking what appeared to be an older married friend about relationships, dating, and marriage. It was evident by the answer that the married friend was not a committed and faithful Christian. Her response was, "Just sleep around for a while. You have plenty of time to be married. You need to experience a lot of different people."

This advice is not only destructive to the girl for today but will negatively impact her future marriage. There could not be worse advice for marriage, but it is the advice the world provides. Because godly individuals base their advice on the eternal and the ungodly base their advice on the temporal, they will never be in exact alignment. The paradigms of the godly and the ungodly will never be the same.

Next, the scripture says blessed is the man that does not stand in the way of sinners. "Standing in the way" means hanging out or just being present where sinners are. Who are sinners? They are those who are condemned as criminals. These individuals are considered less appalling than ungodly. The sinner category can include Christians who are not living according to the scripture. Let this soak in—Christians who are living according to the world have a skewed perspective. As people, we are wired to justify our behaviors. Because of that, Christians living outside of Christ's reign are going to see the world in a way that justifies their behavior. They will develop a version of Christianity that either accommodates or excuses their behavior. That being said, people who do not stand in their midst or on their path or in their hangouts are blessed.

The third blessing comes from not sitting in the seat of

the scornful. *Scornful* is translated to "arrogant." It can also be translated as "judgmental." In other words, godly people should not even sit with those who see themselves as superior to others. The arrogant have become their own gods.

What is the first thing listed in Proverbs 6:16–19 as behavior that God hates or is an abomination to him? It is a proud look, which refers to arrogance. Sitting in the seat of the scornful can be a passive position of just sitting with judgmental people. It can also mean putting ourselves in the place of judgment where we can judge others' actions.

Do you see the progression in the types of people here with whom godly people are advised not to hang out? Yes, it is easy to understand that it is dangerous to our faith to hang out with those who are actively fighting against God. But the psalmist takes it a step further by saying to not even hang around with those who are doing wrong. These are the people who are not fighting against God but are being disobedient. Finally, he takes it even one step further by saying not to stay around those who are arrogant. The arrogant are those who do not even give God time. These are the three levels of disbelief: animosity, disobedience, and apathy. If godly people spends too much time around those exhibiting these beliefs, their faith will diminish.

The progression in attitudes toward God is not the only progression detailed in this passage. Notice that the first part is active: Do not move with or on the advice of the ungodly. It is also more temporary. It is a warning not to move in the direction given by one who is ungodly.

The second part is less active because it states that we shouldn't even stand in the way, area, or behaviors of the sinner. While standing seems more passive, it is also more permanent. We are not to align our positions with those who are living in a way that does not glorify God.

Finally, the behavior becomes even more passive and more fixed: Do not even sit in the midst of them. Don't act like them, don't be in the middle of the group, and don't even passively hang around or set yourself up to be like them. This is hard. Before any of us came to Christ, we were in the category of ungodly. Many of us came to Christ as children and became Christians who were content living in the world among disobedient people. Our society is based on tolerance, so it is very difficult to be in the world without being *of* the world. Besides this, many of us, through our accomplishments or our piety, have become judgmental. It is essential to understand that this transition of focus is difficult to make.

How do we know that this is hard? We know because Jesus prayed about this specifically in John 17:14–19. He asked God to protect us as we move from being children of the world to children of God who are sanctified or made holy through the truth, which is Jesus. Every action, when removed, must be replaced by a different action, or it leaves a void. I remember when my father decided to give up smoking. He didn't just quit. He took up Tootsie Roll Pops. He replaced one behavior with another. That way, he was able to give up the negative behavior of smoking.

The verse does indicate a favorable reward for those who are able to change. For the godly to be blessed, they must replace their prior actions with new activities. So instead of hanging with all of the people who are not living as God has designed, godly people will take joy and find happiness in studying the law of the Lord. Don't misunderstand this. We are not talking about the Ten Commandments. We are talking about the entirety of the law. I know, it is a lot, but Jesus does a great job of summarizing it. When asked what the most important commandments are, Jesus named two commandments. The first is that we are supposed to love God with all our hearts, souls, and might. This is part of the Shema that was given to the Jewish people as their daily prayer in Deuteronomy 6:4–9. The rest of the Shema reminds the children of God to keep these ideas before them in every aspect of life. The other commandment Jesus named is to love others as we love ourselves. Blessed people think about how to serve God and humankind both day and night. You may be wondering just what blessed people get by doing these things.

There is a reward that goes with Psalm 1:1–3:

> Blessed is the man Who walks not in the counsel of the ungodly, Nor stands in the path of sinners, Nor sits in the seat of the scornful; But his delight is in the law of the LORD, And in His law he meditates day and night. He shall be like a tree Planted by the rivers of water, That brings forth its fruit in its season, Whose leaf also shall not wither; And whatever he does shall prosper.

What this means is that such people will have deep roots. When the floods of life come against them, they will not be washed away or moved. We have a creek on the property line behind our house and have seen a couple of substantial floods. There are several trees on either side of the creek. In the last flood, after the waters subsided, it was very clear that one of the trees had not developed a deep root system because it had been completely uprooted and moved downstream. While the flood was a pretty good one, the high waters of the creek should not have been able to uproot it. All of the other trees, the ones with deep roots, were completely unaffected by the rushing waters. Christians who are rooted in the law will not be uprooted when the storms of life hit. Another thing about the tree is that it should produce fruit. Wherever Christians who delight in the law go, they will be making more people like them. You do understand that the fruit contains the seed that replicates the tree. Children of God who live according to the scripture make more children of God as they go on their way. Just like it is the nature of a tree to bear fruit, it is the nature of children of God to bring about more children of God.

Keep in mind that there is a timing issue. The tree will bring forth fruit in its time. As people, we expect to bring forth fruit all of the time. This is just not possible. There are seasons for rest and seasons for bearing fruit. God's time may not be our time. Do not be frustrated if you don't see results immediately.

This verse goes on to say that the leaves of that tree will not wilt. This is important. Leaves on a plant wilt when it does not receive the nourishment it needs. If people stay focused on the law of the Lord, they will be nourished. The last part of the verse says that everything these people touch will prosper.

It seems that we may have corrupted the meaning of the word *prosper* to make it mean what we want it to mean. It means to develop and accomplish the purpose for which something is created. When God prospers a person, he brings to fruition the plan he has for that person's life. So when people protects their minds and hearts and focus on the law of the Lord, God will make sure that they become exactly what he planned for them to be. Please do not think this refers to a financially wealthy or carefree life. Jesus lived this verse perfectly, and from the scripture, we can see his life was not carefree, problem-free, or marked by wealth.

Our thoughts and behaviors go together. The environments in which we allow ourselves to be will determine our thoughts, and our thoughts will determine our behaviors. If people actively protect what becomes a part of their thoughts by watching how and with whom they spend their time and taking action to focus on God and others, they will be strengthened and their vessels will become stronger.

Romans 12:2, which we have already touched on, goes hand in hand with Psalm 1:1–3. Romans tells us not to be molded by the world but to transform ourselves through renewing our minds. Let's talk about renewing. It is the act of making something new again. Is it possible for anything to be made new again? For example, if I buy a car that is twenty years old, can I make it new again? The answer is no. I can't make it new, but I can make it like new. I can take out all of the inner workings of the car and replace them. I can sand the paint down to the metal, repair the rusted areas, and repaint. I can rip out all of the upholstery and redo the entire inside of the car. I can make it like new, but the reality is that it is an old car. People will argue that the renewing of the mind is like the refurbishing of an old car. It may have newer, better thoughts, but the old frame is still there. Good news, Christian—the scripture says we can be made new. Our minds are made new by following the instructions in Philippians 4:8, which tells us to focus on things that are true, honorable, pure, lovely, commendable, excellent, and worthy of praise.

In other words, focus on the gift of salvation and the law of the Lord. Nothing is more worthy of praise than these. Focusing on the gift of salvation reminds of who we are and what God has done for us. It is the well from which eternal hope springs, and this hope provides a way for the mind to be renewed. As the child of God focuses on the law of the Lord, the mind will be made new. This newness of the mind is protection against the wickedness of the world. Just as people learn to spot counterfeit money by looking at real money, people who focus on the truth in the scripture will see the lies of the world. Once those false ideas that look to be the truth are detected, the committed person is able to make better choices based on God's guidelines, not humankind's. The reality is that people rooted in the knowledge of their salvation and the Word of God become impervious to the outside forces.

In relation to developing a tenacious faith, for people who spend time renewing their minds by thinking on the law of God and protect their thoughts by being careful about how and with whom they spend their time, they will be more able to focus on what scripture says than what they see happening before them. I am not going to lie or sugarcoat this: Being a Christian is hard. Jesus said that the world hated him and will hate his followers as well.

Because of this, Christians need to get ready. In times of trials or grief, it is easy to focus on what we see before us and forget what we know about God. When we allow ourselves to be ruled by what we see instead of what we know, we lose our ability to be lights in a dark world. What we allow to rule us will guide our behavior and transform us.

Romans 12:2 does not end with a call to be transformed by the world but to be transformed through the renewing of the mind. It ends with explaining why this is so important. We must do this so we can prove what the will of God is. Children of God can only prove the will of God through standing in faith through adversity.

Think about the tenacity of the bulldog. A bulldog is not deterred by the size or strength of the bull, the risk involved, or the seeming impossibility of the task. That bulldog is motivated by the one thing it was bred to do: to take down that bull.

Christians living as impervious beings in this world should not be motivated by the size of the obstacle, the risk involved, or the looming possibility of defeat. We should be driven only by the purpose for which we were created. First and foremost, that is to worship and fellowship with God. Second, it is to fulfill the call to evangelism. Honestly, Christians who move forward with a do-or-die attitude, who are not deterred by what they see or hear, are going to be the ones who prove the will of God.

EIGHT

OBEDIENT

Be ye doers of the word and not hearers
only, deceiving yourselves. For if
anyone is a hearer of the word and not
a doer, he is like a man observing his
natural face in a mirror for he observes
himself, goes away, and immediately
forgets what kind of man he was.
—James 1:22–24

I am lucky enough to have raised a teenage daughter. Life with Sarah was fun because we had girls in our house all of the time. The funny thing is that at the bottom of our front staircase hangs a mirror, and over several years of watching the girls ascend and descend the stairs, it is clear that they stop to look in that mirror more often than not. It doesn't matter if they have just left the bathroom mirror upstairs; there is always one last glance in the mirror on the stairs before leaving the house. I have thought about this a lot, partially because I too use that mirror more often than I want to admit.

Also, it seems that I am always a little startled when I

look in the mirror. In my mind, I am the twenty-something who is still young and attractive. In reality, I am a fifty-something who doesn't always recognize the woman in the mirror. Because of this, I think I understand what the book of James is telling us. When we look in the mirror and walk away, we think of ourselves not as we appear but as we want to appear. We lie to ourselves, thinking we are much better than we are.

James 1:22–25 says that when we just listen to God's Word but don't do it, we are like the man who looks at his face in the mirror, walks away, and forgets how he looks. When we just hear the Word of God but do not act, we are lulled into a false belief that everything is okay. We forget that we have a sinful nature and that we live in a sinful world at war with God. Those who are only hearers of the Word can adopt the false mentality of "I'm okay, and you're okay." Children of God who are hearers only forget that they are called by God to be different.

As we have seen through the previous chapters, there is no part of being a Christian that aligns with what the world believes or is doing. The opposite of the people who go to church yet still live by the world's standards are the people who are doers of the word. Because they are actively looking at the perfect law and doing it, they do not forget who they are or who they are called to be. Because they are actively living the Word of God, it becomes their identity. Think about how people connect their identities to their actions.

My dad, although he did many things, loved being a cowboy. He loved going to the ranch, feeding the cows, and gathering the sheep. You get my drift. When it became clear that he was getting ready to be with the Lord, he wrote out what he wanted on his headstone. Those few words say everything about how he saw himself. If you go out to the cemetery and look at his gravestone, you will see "Homer Hilton 'Bud' Stephens, Ranch Hand for the Lord." He saw his job on earth as tending to the Lord's flock as he worked on the Lord's land.

When I taught college and people asked me about my job, instead of saying I was a professor, I said I was a teacher of teachers. Even for the short time that I spent as an executive in the private sector, I called myself a teacher. What we do, our actions, becomes our identity. This scripture from the book of James is explicit that those who only listen will deceive themselves, but those who study the law and follow through will be blessed by doing so. Keep in mind that the law is based on loving God with all your heart, soul, and mind. If we, as Christians, focus on this, we will know who we are and to whom we belong.

Why is it important to understand to whom we belong? It is because knowing our relationship to God gives us strength and an ability to go before him for help. My dad used to tell a story about a Union soldier who tried many times to get an audience with President Lincoln. His father and brother had both been killed in the war, and he wanted to ask permission to return home to bury his family members and stay with his mother to provide her comfort and help. However, every time he tried to speak to the president, he was turned away. One day, after trying and being refused, he went to sit on a park bench across from the White House and started crying. As his tears flowed down his cheeks, a little boy appeared and asked what was wrong. The soldier recounted his story to the young boy.

Once he had finished his tale, the boy took him by the hand and said, "Come with me."

The soldier, holding the child's hand, walked back across the street, up the sidewalk, past the guards, into the White House, and stepped inside the doors of the Oval Office, where he was introduced to President Lincoln by his son, Tad. You see, Tad knew who he was, and he knew he could get an audience with the president at any point. We need to know who we are, and we can know that only by hearing the Word of God and doing it. In case you want to look for this story, I couldn't find a historical basis for it. As I stated, my dad used to tell this story. Although I am not sure if it is true, it does make the point.

Jesus himself explained what it is to hear the words of God and do them. In Luke 6:46, he asked his disciples why they would call him Lord if they weren't going to do what he told them to do. That is a fair question. If you call him Lord and don't follow his commands, it is lip service only; therefore, he isn't really Lord. He says that if you obey him, you are like the man who, when building a house, sets a firm foundation on the rock. For the house on a strong foundation, the storms will come and the floods will pound against the house, but the house will not be moved.

Let's consider the opposite of this. If you call Jesus Lord but do not follow his words, you are like the man who builds his house on a faulty foundation. When the storms of life come against it, the house will be pushed wherever the raging flood chooses. Think about this. You are only stable if you are obedient.

I cannot count how often the storms of life came when I was young in my faith and disobedient, and I was utterly unable to navigate them because my life was at the mercy of the rising waves. It was terrifying. I can remember calling out to God and begging him to save me from the mess I had made.

Although he did save me, I generally got to go through the storms and their aftermath. You see, God loves us enough to let us learn from the storms. He protected me so I could live to make the right decision and repent, but he did not always protect me from the pain of my disobedience. As I have become more obedient and steadfast in my faith, the storms have become more violent and had a higher possibility of destruction.

The exciting thing is that because I am focused on loving God with all my heart, soul, and might, the foundation of my faith is not at all shaken. In fact, people often think everything is easy for me because I am seldom rattled. I will tell you that my strength and peace are a result of only focusing on God's Word and doing it. As I have learned to be obedient, I have become more aware of who I am called to be, and my foundation is firm.

There is more to the blessing of obedience than just knowing who you are, whose you are, and having a foundation. An element of protection is found in obedience. Think about it this way: God did not create rules just to create them. He established rules or laws to protect his children, much like parents develop rules to protect their children. When I was a young child, my parents had a few rules, like don't go in the street, hold hands when we walk across the parking lot, and stay together when at the store. If my sister and I did these things, we were less likely to be injured, taken, or killed. The purpose of the rules was to provide a hedge of protection.

The same is true with the laws that God has commanded.

If we focus on loving him and others, we are less likely to do things that harm ourselves or others. For example, if I am focused on loving God and my spouse and doing only things to honor them, I won't do something that will ultimately destroy my marriage. If I am focused on loving and honoring God and honoring my employer, I won't do things that will harm my career. If I am focused on loving and honoring God and loving my neighbor as myself, I won't do something that could harm relationships and cause hard feelings. Now, hear me on this—you can do everything right and still have your marriage fall apart, lose your job, and experience discord in your neighborhood. The difference is that you will have the ability to stand on the knowledge of who you are and that you did your part in the right way. Obedience does lessen the likelihood of things going bad.

There is one concept regarding obedience that we need to address: our obedience or our works do not save us. We are saved by grace. In other words, we do not find salvation through obedience; we find obedience through salvation. Obedience is the result of a loving Savior working in our hearts. As we develop our relationship with the Lord and draw closer to him, we will honor him with our lives.

I remember my first job as a teacher. I knew that the principal, James Brasher, had taken some significant chances to hire me. As I went through the district training, I could see him doing whatever he could to make my transition from student teacher to teacher easier. Because of his sacrifices, I would have done anything not to disappoint him. How much more significant is the gift of salvation that Christ provides than the gift of transition given by my principal? When we can understand the gift of salvation, which is much greater than anything we can experience, the only appropriate response is obedience.

Occasionally, Christians like me want to follow Christ and call him Lord but are a little slow in figuring out the obedience part. We are all about grace without the judgment that comes as a result of disobedience. We are like unruly little lambs. Because the shepherds of biblical times watched their sheep in open fields, they had ways of dealing with unruly lambs. It was vital for the survival of the sheep that they stay close to the shepherd.

Most sheep remain with the herd and the shepherd, but from time to time, an unruly lamb is born. This sheep runs off and gets into trouble, and the shepherd has to leave the herd to go in search of it. It is clear that the one sheep puts itself in danger and also endangers the rest of the herd.

When this occurred the shepherd would take drastic measures: he would break one leg of the unruly lamb. I know it sounds barbaric. He would then bind the leg and carry the lamb everywhere he went. He would take the lamb to fresh grass and clear water and sleeps with it, and the lamb, in turn, grew attached to the shepherd and would no longer wander.

As I look back over my life, I can see times when Jesus, the Good Shepherd, had no other choice but to break me and make me dependent on him. Although those life experiences were painful, they demonstrated to me the lengths that Christ was willing to carry me so that I would become willing to follow him. Out of those times of heartbreak and brokenness, the desire to be obedient developed.

Obedience impacts faith in several ways. First, obedience ensures that we are on the right path and putting our faith in the right thing. I hear people saying they trust God to do this or that, but it doesn't happen. I do not believe God's refusal to answer is the result of a lack of faith on the part of the believer. As Christians, we sometimes pray for God to provide a miracle that will not bring us closer to him or his will for us.

I think God is too good of a father to give us something that we don't need. I cannot tell you how many times I have prayed for something that I didn't get only to find out later that if I had gotten what I prayed for, it would have been utterly destructive. People living in disobedience will have a difficult time developing faith because it will always feel like God is working against them. Just for the record, he may be working to bring them back to him.

The development of an obedient heart gives a person the strength to stand when it doesn't seem possible. What do I know about this? I know that in my most significant times of heartbreak, I go back to the scripture.

Because the Word of God tells me to praise God through my tears, I praise God. Because the scripture instructs me to offer grace to my persecutors, I forgive. Because the Bible tells me that what I have in Christ is so much better than I deserve, I can stand when it appears that I would lose everything. In fact, because I have decided to be obedient regardless of what I experience, people can see my faith in God and be inspired to keep going during their times of trouble.

You may be wondering if God always saves me from pain, embarrassment, or failure. The answer is no. Has he used the things that hurt me badly to create opportunities for others to find him through my witness? Yes. At this point, my goal is to be so determined to be obedient that any obstacle thrown at me becomes irrelevant. In doing this, others can see how to keep going during times of trouble and pain.

Along with strength, obedience brings purpose. All of the disciples left their homes, families, jobs, and dreams of the future to follow the carpenter who was also an itinerate preacher. Their obedience cost them everything, but it also gave their lives a purpose they could have never conceived.

While I agree that their relationship with Jesus gave them the strength to be obedient, it was their obedience that made everything they went through purposeful. The reality is that when people submit to God's will, their lives are directed by the Creator of the universe. When they understand that there is a purpose for every experience they have, it produces an incredible strength to hold onto faith even in the most challenging times.

My dad used to say that Christianity is not for sissies or the faint of heart. Neither is obedience. Being obedient to God may require that you walk through the Valley of the Shadow of Death. It may require you to build a boat in the desert. It may require you to sacrifice everything. Remember Abraham, who had tenacious faith waiting for over twenty-five years to have a son? Well, let's skip ahead to when that child was a teenager. God spoke to Abraham and told him to take his son up on a specific mountain and sacrifice him. If I were Abraham, I would have a problem with this request. First of all, I wouldn't want to do it. Second, I wouldn't want to have to explain to Sarah what had happened to her only son. Where this would be a problem for me, it wasn't for Abraham. Abraham told Isaac, "Come on, kid. I need you to carry this wood. We are going to that mountain over there to make a sacrifice to God." Isaac picked up the wood and walked side by side with his father to the mountain.

Can you imagine the thoughts that must have been going through Abraham's mind as he walked by his son? As they walked up the mountain, Isaac said, basically, "Hey, Pops, I see the wood and the rope, but where is the sacrifice?" I can imagine Abraham saying, "God will provide" as his heart shattered inside his chest. They got to the top of the mountain, and Abraham bound Isaac and placed him on the altar. At this point, Isaac certainly realized that his father intended to kill him.

I don't know if he pleaded with his father, but his eyes must have reflected fear. As Abraham lifted his arm to drive the dagger into his child, God intervened. God provided a ram with its horns caught in a thicket of thorns. He told Abraham to cut Isaac loose and sacrifice the ram instead.

From that experience, Abraham's faith that God would provide must have become a driving force in his life. Abraham's obedience built his faith, and it had to have impacted the faith of his son. Isaac saw firsthand what total sacrifice meant and how God could and would intervene.

Obedience truly opens doors for God to work, but it also gives us the strength and purpose to stand firm while the storm rages all around. As we have discovered, without obedience, Christians do not know who they are, do not have a foundation, and cannot stand firm in a storm. Without obedience, faith has nothing in which to take root.

NINE

UNRESTRAINED

Then Mary took a pound of very
costly oil of spikenard, anointed the
feet of Jesus, and wiped his feet with
her hair. And the house was filled
with the fragrance of the oil.
—John 12:3

As I was thinking about what it means to be unrestrained, I realized the word *unrestrained* is another way of saying "without boundaries." Think of it this way—many years ago, my father discovered that he needed a way of hauling fencing materials to and from locations where his truck could not go because either the path was too narrow or the brush was too dense.

He decided the best way to do this was to purchase a mule and a wagon. It would be easy to load the new fencing materials onto the wagon, lead the mule hitched up to the wagon to the area where the fence needed to be rebuilt, and load the old fence materials up at the end of the day. With his mind made up, my dad headed to the auction barn where animals like cows, horses, and mules were sold. It just so happened that the auction had one mule for sale. My dad took one look at that mule and knew she was perfect for the job, so he bought her.

On his way to the ranch with the mule, Dad called a friend who had a little wagon and a harness and arranged for his friend to bring the items and meet him at the ranch. They both arrived and were as excited as two children at Christmas. They unloaded the mule and put the harness on her with no problems. Thinking this was an excellent idea, they attached the wagon. Once the wagon was connected to the harness, the mule's ears perked up; she stopped her grazing; and with one jump, she and the wagon headed east as fast as her legs could carry her. Dad's immediate thought was that she would stop when she got to the fence. He was incorrect. The mule, wagon and all, went through the fence without even slowing down. She kept going and disappeared into the brush of the neighboring ranch. She was found about three weeks later, two ranches over with only the harness intact. You see, that mule, once she was fired up, was unrestrained. Nothing could stop her.

How does this translate into loving God in an unrestrained way, erasing or ignoring all possible boundaries? After all, the Shema—the prayer that the Jews were told to pray twice daily—includes Deuteronomy 6:5, which says, "You shall love the Lord your God with all your heart, with all your soul, and with all your might." This verse means that we are to love God with all we are and without boundaries. We will look at a couple of examples found in scripture that demonstrate an unrestrained love for Christ.

The first account is found in Luke 7:36–50. In this account, Jesus was asked to eat at the house of a Pharisee.

He accepted the invitation. Of course, the news of Jesus going to eat at the Pharisee's house spread like wildfire. A woman who made her living in ways that were less than reputable heard of this lunch date and decided to go see Jesus. She wasn't going just to see him but to honor him. This account is of her offering. Jesus arrived at the house of Simon the Pharisee. Although Simon should have greeted Jesus at the door with a kiss, there was no welcome kiss for this guest. Although a servant should have been at the door with a bowl of water to wash the feet of Jesus, there was no servant or washing of feet.

Although Simon treated Jesus as less than a guest, Jesus sat down at the table to share a meal with him. While Jesus was eating, the woman who was a sinner entered the house. Although it was customary for uninvited visitors to "crash" meetings with special guests, it was not the norm for a woman such as this one to enter the house of a Pharisee. She looked around, spotted Jesus, stood behind him, and began to weep.

Although the only people mentioned as being present are the Pharisee, the woman, and Jesus, there would have been more people, if only the servants. The woman uncovered her head and unpinned her hair. As her hair fell, a hush fell over the room. She bowed down and covered the Lord's feet with tears and kisses. Then she used her hair, her crowning glory, to wipe the dirty, damp feet of Jesus. I'm sure there was a gasp as the woman produced an alabaster flask of costly scented ointment and began to anoint the Lord's feet.

By this point, everyone in the room was in shock—everyone except the woman and Jesus. Of course, the host was likely rethinking his choice to invite Jesus over. He must have wondered how this itinerant preacher could be a prophet if he allowed this unclean woman to touch him.

Let's take a break from the story for a minute and look at the barriers this woman broke as she demonstrated unrestrained love. First, she broke religious barriers. Because of who she was, she was not welcome in the Pharisee's home. She of all people understood the risk here. She was going to walk into the home of the person who condemned her the most.

Because Jesus was a guest of the Pharisee, she could expect him also to reject her in this environment. This woman walked into a situation where she knew that she would be scorned and judged. She set herself up to be mocked and condemned by the townspeople where she lived for as long as she lived. This woman would be more than shunned; she would be ridiculed by those involved in this event, who would keep her forever from the temple.

She also broke social barriers. For the woman to uncover her head and take down her hair showed complete humility and submission. It was a shocking event because, in a sense, it was akin to nakedness. Covering the head in the Jewish culture is a sign of modesty; she removed her covering. She allowed herself to be vulnerable not only before Jesus but before everyone else present. Also, she used her hair, which was the most glorious part of her, to dry the filthiest part of Jesus, his feet. She took the place of the servant or slave.

Third, she broke financial barriers. The gift she gave was extravagant! An alabaster box of ointment was considered extremely expensive, and it had a special meaning. Consider that in biblical times it was common for the family of a woman who had come of age to buy an alabaster box and fill it with perfumed ointment. The ointment in the box was equal to the woman's worth and displayed her family's wealth. In essence, this woman poured her worth onto the feet of Jesus. Once the ointment was gone, she was valueless. This ointment was intended to be used to anoint her groom's feet and bring honor to him. She was coming to give Jesus not only her past and present but also her future.

In today's environment, what does it look like to break the religious, social, and financial barriers to love Jesus in an unrestrained way? While I certainly don't have all of the answers here, I have experienced a few things that might be helpful. In our world of multidenominations and varying beliefs within denominations, the list of barriers that could be broken is innumerable. I know that, in searching for a right relationship with God, you may find yourself at a crossroads with your denomination or religious group.

Keep in mind that God will never ask you to do something that violates his two greatest commandments: to love your Lord with all your heart, soul, and might and to love others as you love yourself. Some of the traditions and customs are subject to interpretation. I have written about how God got my attention when I was in college. During that time, I believed that he was calling me to seek a bachelor's degree in Bible. Honestly, this was not entirely popular with the university or my fellow students. I have often joked that my classmates saw me as either a heretic or a lunatic. The reality is that God needed me to be educated in a way that would allow me to interpret scripture on a historical and linguistic basis. I would never have learned that in any other degree path. So, there I was, a woman going against what my denomination supported. It was uncomfortable and stressful, and it demanded that I be wholly committed to staying the course. Although it may have appeared to the religious leaders in my life that I was way off track, I was doing what God needed me to do to be prepared for what he was going to call me to do.

Social barriers also abound and will have to be broken. Having spent over ten years in the world of higher education, I am no stranger to the aversion of many in the academic world to any form of faith, Christian or otherwise. I worked in a department that included Christians, atheists, agnostics, and people of multiple other religions. I remember walking into a room and hearing one of my fellow professors talking about the weak-minded, bigoted Christians. I was stunned to hear that perspective of Christianity. I also remember being in my doctoral training and being told by the dean of the college of education that if he heard me talking about Jesus, he would ensure that I would never graduate. So in these situations, what do you do? I prayed and let God open the doors that he wanted me to go through. I remember sitting in diversity training at work several weeks after my colleague commented on Christians. Each of us was asked to fill in the blanks on a paper that said, "I am a _____ but I am not a _____." I wrote, "I am a Christian, but I am not a small-minded bigot." When the leader of the seminar asked who would share, I raised my hand. Not only was I asked to share my information, but I was also allowed to explain the plan of salvation to a group of people who did not understand or respect Christianity. I wish I could say that it went perfectly and people believed. While my colleagues were respectful, they weren't receptive.

As far as the dean who told me not to mention Jesus,

God had a plan for that. After my father died, I returned to my doctoral program. At that point, I was a teaching assistant. The day I arrived back on campus, the dean announced that he would go with me to my first teaching assignment. He further instructed me to tell my students about the difficulties I had leading up to my father's death to encourage them to overcome obstacles in their lives.

Through tears punctuated by uncontrollable sobs, I told my story. Then a miracle happened. A student in the middle of the room raised her hand and asked, "How did you make it? I mean, you had so much going on. How did you do it?" My eyes met those of the dean; he gave a half-smile and nodded his head to say yes. I answered, "Jesus carried me." More questions about my relationship with Jesus were asked, and I answered each one.

As my dean and I walked back to his office, he answered my unasked question. He said, "If they ask you, you can openly tell them. I will never stop you." For the next ten years, I told my story in every class every semester. Every time I told it, God provided a student to ask me how I survived. God can even break down social barriers.

You may be curious about financial barriers. I am finding ways that God is challenging me to go beyond my boundary of financial comfort. When my daughter felt like she was being called to summer ministry in China, I knew it was the right thing. Because it was in China, many of our family members believed it was too dangerous and would not help support the trip. I worked with her as we watched God provide the funds. She did her part—she prepared, sacrificed, and saved her money, and God provided where she fell short.

It has been that way over and over in the lives of Christians. My dad used to say, "God doesn't send you out to fix the fence without supplies and tools. Just pick up what you can and head in the direction you've been sent, and you will find he is with you carrying the rest." Ministry and service do not belong to us. They belong to God, and he is wholly vested in going out and changing people.

If he calls you to show your love for him in a financially uncomfortable way, just do it. He is the master of making things happen. Despite our beliefs that we are an integral part of everything, he can do this without our help. Because he loves us, he allows us to participate in what he is doing.

Along with loving God in an unrestrained way, we are called to live in an unrestrained way. Hebrews 12:1 says, "Therefore we also, since we are surrounded by so great a cloud of witnesses, let us lay aside every weight, and the sin which so easily ensnares us, and let us run with endurance the race that is set before us."

Remember that mule that my dad bought? When we found her, she was missing the wagon. She had thrown off the burden in her run. That was not an easy task; we found pieces of wagon scattered over two different pastures. The fact is that that mule ran until the burden no longer existed.

Folks, life is incredibly difficult, but this passage lets us know that we are not alone. We have a cloud of witnesses. Believe it or not, they are cheering for us to make it. They believe that despite everything life throws at us, we will be successful. When we fall, they yell for us to get up and keep running. They also are screaming for the other runners to help us up. Occasionally I hear of runners giving up the win to help another runner cross the finish line. I can only imagine that the crowd of witnesses is cheering for others to help us but for us to help others as well.

That is not all—we are told that we are to run the race unrestrained because this crowd is watching us. We are instructed to lay aside every weight and sin that easily entangles us and slows us down. One of the best literary portrayals of sin is found in Charles Dickens's *A Christmas Carol*. In it, Ebenezer Scrooge is visited by the ghost of his departed business partner Marley. Marley is draped in heavy chains representing his sins and wrongdoings. Let's take this image to the race of life. If you were wrapped in heavy chains of sin, how well would you run? We know the answer. You cannot run while bound by sin. To run the race, we must ask Christ to cut us free from arrogance, gossip, stirring up discord, lying, thinking of wickedness, and judging, along with all of the other sins, to be able to run the race.

We also have to put down any burdens that might get in our way. Think about your burdens as rocks you carry. The burdens of personal dreams and aspirations, financial concerns, social constructs, religious expectations, and family expectations may all have to be thrown to the side. How fast and how far can you run with your arms full of rocks? I know for myself that running the race without the additional burdens is going to be hard enough. I cannot do it with chains and rocks.

As I am writing this, I am overwhelmed with some of the things that I need to lay aside. Like everyone else, I have been hurt by people I trust. I have to decide whether to pick up that rock of hurt feelings or throw it to the side. I have a fear of failure, which is another way of saying I have an ego. Am I going to try to run carrying that rock or let it go? What about concerns about meeting the expectations of others? I just don't think I want to keep carrying that rock.

I need to make decisions about my lifestyle that will allow me to set down the rock of financial worry. I need to put rocks down. In addition to the stones, there are chains of sin that I need Jesus's help to cut off and leave off. These are my convictions; you may find you have some things that no longer have a place in your life as you begin to focus on the race that is set before you.

Like it or not, we are all on the track. Some of us are running, some are walking, and some are lying down. If you are in the running crowd, you are doing what is expected. If you are in the walking group, as long as you are headed in the right direction, you are making progress. Although I believe that walking is not the best option, I know that I have had to walk a couple of laps in life because I was either too tired or injured to run. If you are in the group that is lying down on the track, you, my friend, are a stumbling block. As Christians, this is not an option. Christians who are lying down are people who know Christ but are not living for him. They are satisfied with keeping their knowledge a secret. They are causing everyone who knows and respects them to stumble.

Let's keep in mind that running unrestrained means not being weighed down by other things or restrained by oneself. In this race, we don't know where the end is. Our job is to run for all we are worthwhile we can run.

An unrestrained life is not a safe life. It is open to criticism and judgment from the rest of the world. Have you ever noticed that no one criticizes people who are not in the race? Only those on the track, running in the lead, are criticized. No one really has much to say about those who are status quo.

Like the woman who gave it all, it is up to us to

determine how much of our value we are willing to pour on the feet of Jesus. Like the person in the race, we have to decide what things of value we are willing to put down to do our best. Like the old mule of my dad's, we have to determine which barriers will not become roadblocks to moving forward. You see, tenacious faith is easy when the only thing that counts is Jesus.

TEN

SELFLESS

Then Jesus said to His disciples,
"If anyone desires to come after
Me, let him deny himself, and take
up his cross, and follow me."
—Matthew 16:24

I know how to be a lot of things. I know how to be kind, generous, competitive, and diligent, but I'm not sure if I can be selfless. Being selfless is beyond difficult. Why wouldn't it be? One of the basic instincts of any animal, human or otherwise, is self-preservation. Like it or not, we are born with an innate desire to do whatever it takes to ensure our existence. Being selfless goes against our nature, logic, and intellect. It also goes against our culture that tells us we have to take care of ourselves because no one else will. I believe Matthew 16:24 is one of the "hard sayings" of Jesus. In this verse, Jesus says, "If anyone desires to come after Me, let him deny himself, and take up his cross, and follow Me."

Human nature and culture tell us that the focus of life is to meet our own needs and live life how we want to, the way that feels good. In this saying, Jesus was not just addressing behaviors like denying oneself; he was changing the focus of life. The new center, according to Matthew 16:24, is Jesus. Instead of enjoying life, following Jesus becomes the focus. It is essential to understand that a person cannot have two points of focus; for people to adopt a new focus, they must let go of the old one.

What does Jesus mean by "come after me"? Some say it just means to follow Jesus, but it is so much more than that. This phrase is the same type of call a teacher or a prophet would issue to someone who would be a student or trainee. We can see how this works in the story of Elijah calling Elisha. The actual story is found in 1 Kings 19:19–21. The prophet, Elijah, had been instructed to anoint Elisha as the next prophet. Elijah found Elisha plowing the field using a team of twelve oxen. Elijah went up to him and threw his cloak around Elisha.

All of the people reading this text understand the symbolism of this act. Placing one's cloak around another person is a part of creating a covenant. The cloak represents the identity of the one who owns it. What Elijah was saying to Elisha and everyone else was that when people saw Elisha, they would see Elijah. In other words, Elijah was taking responsibility for Elisha.

How did Elisha respond to Elijah and the call to follow and become his student? He accepted the invitation and burned any bridges that would allow him to go back to his old life. Specifically, Elisha took the twelve oxen that he was plowing with and slaughtered them. Next, he built a fire with the wood from the plow and cooked the oxen. Before he left, he fed all of the people with the meat.

You may be wondering if Elisha understood what he

was being called to accomplish. The last part of verse 21 lets us know that Elisha knew what his new position would be: "Then he rose up and followed Elijah, and became his servant." Although Elisha understood that he would one day take Elijah's place, he also understood that he had to become his servant first.

When you feel Jesus tugging at your heart, you sense his part of the promise. He is throwing his cloak around you so that when others see you, they see him. It is essential to understand that, once you accept the cloak or identity of Jesus, God will see you through Jesus. The act of wrapping you in a cloak provides another image of how Jesus willingly covers your sin and makes you acceptable to God.

Your response to him has two parts. First, you must be willing to destroy any means of going back to the life you had before he wrapped you in his cloak. Second, you are to stand up and make yourself the servant. How to become a servant is explained in the three steps that Jesus provides; one must deny himself, take up his cross, and follow Christ.

Let's focus on what it means to deny the self. Our culture tells us that denying oneself is choosing not to watch the extra episode of your Netflix binge or deciding not to eat the additional cookie. It is more than that. Imagine an ornate throne in the throne room in the middle of a fantastic kingdom. Each morning, King Self arises and takes his place upon the throne. From that place, he makes decisions regarding how the kingdom's wealth is spent, what duties are most important, and how the kingdom progresses. One day, King Self meets a ruler. This ruler is superior in every way to the king. And King Self knows that if he gives his throne and kingdom to the ruler, he and his kingdom will be better.

There is a throne in the heart of every person. From the time each person is born, he or she sits on the throne of the heart and makes decisions for his or her own life. Occasionally that person seeks counsel from others, but ultimately, the choices he or she makes are based on wants and needs. Then one day, Jesus, a much better ruler, arrives and offers to take over the kingdom. The existing king or queen must decide whether to give up the position of ruler to become a servant to the new king. Even though life will be better and the lives of all who know the current ruler will be enriched, the ruler has to decide to either remain as king or queen or become a servant. This idea of a ruler handing over his or her kingdom is the picture of what it looks like to deny oneself.

With Jesus as king of my heart, I have found things I have to deny to myself. I no longer have the right to judge or punish others for their wrongdoing. If I believe that God is in control of my destiny, then I have to see every event in my life as being allowed by God to move me in the right direction, change me so I am better suited for his needs, or allow me to demonstrate my faith. If I believe God is in control, there is never a reason to hold a grudge or punish people for their misdeeds. I need to demonstrate grace.

The path for my future is not my own but is designed by God. I don't have the option of complaining. I do believe that God can handle my objections and questions; even Jesus asked in Luke 22:42 for the cup to pass, if it was God's will. That being said, I think complaining about what has already happened shows a self-centered, not Christ-centered, attitude.

My job is to serve. As Elisha left his job as a plowboy to become a servant, I abandon my role as king, one I am not qualified for anyway, to take up the position of a servant.

The second step in becoming a servant to the Lord is to take up one's cross, to pick up the burden of self-sacrifice. To be honest, I am not sure how well people understand self-sacrifice. Most people believe this is about abandoning personal ambition and the desire to amass wealth or prestige. In looking at what the disciples gave up, I believe it means pouring out of one's life to serve the Lord. Imagine the burden that Paul picked up to follow Christ. Suddenly, the hunter of Christians became what he had hunted. He gave up his upwardly mobile, influential, and high-paying position to become an itinerate preacher and the unpaid writer of several books in the New Testament. I am not sure we ever fully understand the burden of sacrifice. I know that once committed to Christ, the sacrifice is more of an honor than a burden. You see, servants who live their lives in service to the King live in the King's presence, and that in itself is an honor.

The third step in becoming a servant is in the act of following. I know a lot about following. I am a short little woman with short little legs. I spend a lot of my time following. My husband is continuously looking around to see if I am still with him. A few days ago, we were at Walmart. Bob was walking along, and I was following. We approached an item that Bob was a little interested in, so he stopped to take a look, and I kept walking. Now, you have to understand that Bob had the items for purchase with him. He had the keys to the truck. Ultimately, I was not going anywhere without that man. But I thought I knew where we were going, so I kept walking. Imagine my surprise when I turned around to find that Bob was not behind me. I looked and looked, and there he was, in line to check out. The end of the story is that I scurried back to him, and we walked out together. The point is that it was not my turn to lead. I may have thought I knew the plan, but there were some things that I did not know that changed the plan. We often think we know what God is doing, and we try to run ahead. It never works.

Sometimes, as I did at the store, I focus on things other than Jesus and miss the turn. That is when I have to go back to where I saw Jesus last. That is why it is so essential to stay in constant communication with the Lord. Folks, this is why we are supposed to pray about everything.

When we think about people following the Lord, the disciples are the people who come to mind. Let's take a brief look at what it meant for some of the people who became the daily companions of the Lord to follow him. Let's look at Simon, the man who would become Peter. When the Lord called Simon, he walked away from his fishing boat and nets. He walked away from the world he understood. Because the scripture tells us that Jesus healed Simon Peter's mother-in-law, we know that Simon had a wife. For Simon to follow Jesus, he had to give up control over how he would support his wife and children, if they had any. Simon and his wife had to sacrifice time they would have spent together. I am confident that the physical and emotional sacrifices he made cannot even be counted. Ultimately, he was crucified upside down. Simon Peter sacrificed his time and himself.

The disciple who gave up the most prestige and possessions to follow Christ was Matthew, the tax collector. He went from being a darling of the Roman Empire to being seen as a criminal. He sacrificed all of the creature comforts that could be found during that time for life as a follower of Christ. There were times after he left his job that he was hungry and had no place to lay his head.

When he was a tax collector, Matthew could determine where he would go and what he would do. After he left that position, his life was filled with being a servant of the Lord, providing for others, or serving Christ directly. He would never again have the political prestige and power he once held.

A group of unnamed women also traveled with Jesus and the disciples. We have no way to know what they sacrificed. Most likely, they gave up the traditional Jewish role of mother and grandmother to follow the Lord. If they were not married, they would never be married because many of them used all of their possessions to help provide for the Lord and his disciples.

Some of these women were the mothers of the disciples, and while they certainly gave up the comforts and stability of having a place to call home, there must have been a sweetness to watching their sons transform under the guidance of the Lord. No matter what was gained or lost, all of the disciples and the women would undoubtedly say that the sacrifice was less than the blessing that resulted. The sacrifice deals with the temporal, but the blessing is eternal.

I think sometimes we feel like serving the Lord is something that is just between God and us. In other words, if I am a decent person, praying, and going to church, my boxes are checked and I am okay. This concept is not just a contemporary view; Jesus talks about it in Matthew 25:31–46. The following is my condensed version of the encounter. Jesus basically told his followers, "When I come back, and I will, all of the nations will be brought before me. At that time, I will divide those who are faithful followers from those who aren't. The real followers I will put on my right. Those who are followers in name and not deed will go on my left. Then I will call to those on my right and say, 'Today is your day! Come and inherit the kingdom set aside for you. You tended to all of my needs; you fed me and gave me a drink. You took me in, and you clothed me. You cared for me when I was sick, and you visited me when I was in prison.' The righteous will be puzzled and say, 'Lord, we never saw you hungry or thirsty. I'm pretty sure I never gave you clothes or took you in. I would remember if I cared for you when you were sick, and I know I would remember visiting you in prison.'" I can just imagine the Lord shaking his head and saying, "Oh, my sweet, sweet children. As you ministered to people who were not considered important to society, you ministered to me."

Then he will turn to those on his left and say, "Depart from me into the lake of fire." Those on his left will, in fear and anxiety, say, "But Lord, we went to church at least twice a year. I mean, we went to the building and not just watched it on TV. I know you say that we did not feed you or give you drink or do any other stuff, but can you blame us? We didn't know it was you." Jesus will silence them with a raised hand and send them off to everlasting punishment.

This meaning of this parable is obvious. God will judge us based on our service to him. Remember, we are not saved by our service. Our service is the result of a redeemed life. Our service demonstrates who is the king of our hearts. The way we serve God is through helping others. Although a list is provided here of things that can be done, the intention is not to use it to check the boxes on the list and consider the task complete.

Through this parable, the Lord says that we should be mindful of the human need around us and meet that need. It doesn't take money or prestige to notice someone is upset and comfort them. It is possible to share food or drink with someone who has nothing.

I remember sitting with a friend discussing this passage. My friend was upset because she didn't have a car, so she couldn't help people who were not close to her home. She had made a mental list of all of the things she couldn't do. As she was going through that list with me, I watched her brush and braid a neighbor child's hair. While we were talking, another child from the neighborhood asked if he could use her bathroom because he was locked out of his house. She nodded, smiled, and waved him in. As I was getting ready to leave, an elderly neighbor pulled into the driveway next door. Without skipping a beat, my friend excused herself to help her neighbor out of the car. Without being asked, she grabbed the groceries out of the car and carried them into the house for the older woman. When my friend came back to tell me goodbye, I told her not to worry because I had just watched her meet the needs of those around her, just like she is supposed to. She didn't recognize her service because it just poured out of her.

Jesus didn't give us a list of things to do. He said that if we are his, we will be selfless in meeting the needs of the people around us. We will provide a kind word when it is needed. We will volunteer, drop off food, and take care of those who can't take care of themselves. It isn't about the specific duties; it is about living a life of service. It is crucial to keep in mind that Colossians 3:23 tells us that as we serve, it is to be done as if we are serving the Lord himself.

The last description of being selfless is found in Romans 12:1. Paul writes, "I beseech you therefore, brethren, by the mercies of God, that you present your bodies a living sacrifice, holy, acceptable to God, which is your reasonable service." Have you ever thought about what sacrifice is? In the Old Testament, when an animal sacrifice was made, that animal was killed. Its blood was poured out of it. When Paul wrote that we were to be a living sacrifice, he intentionally used a word that the Jewish people equated with the ultimate offering that can be made to God.

He referred to 1 Samuel 15:22, which would have been a familiar passage to those who frequented the temple: "Has the LORD as great delight in burnt offerings and sacrifices, As in obeying the voice of the LORD? Behold, to obey is better than sacrifice, And to heed than the fat of rams." Those reading Paul's letter to the Romans would connect the living sacrifice with obedience. God doesn't want us to give him stuff. He already has everything. God wants your obedience. He doesn't want the elaborate rituals. He doesn't need incense or memorized liturgies. He doesn't want the sacrifice of grain, first fruits, or animals. God wants you. He wants your heart and life. He wants you like you are. He will help you to work on what needs to be changed. He wants your commitment, your adoration, and your friendship. In short, he wants you to do what my dad did every day after he met Jesus. He wants you to walk with him, share your thoughts and time with him, and be in love with him. With this kind of relationship, the most amazing words one could hope to hear are, "We are closer to my home than yours. Will you come home with me today?"

ELEVEN

NOW WHAT?

Truly my soul silently waits for God;
From Him comes my salvation.
He only is my rock and my salvation;
He is my defense;
I shall not be moved.
—Psalm 62:1–2

I don't know about you, but this whole tenacious-faith living thing seems a little overwhelming. Trying to strengthen my ability to be thankful, evangelical, nonsubjective, authentic, courageous, impervious, obedient, unrestrained, and selfless just seems like a lot. As much as I want to, I am sure that there is no way I am going to be able to get it all together and be the person who can live a truly tenaciously faithful life. Please understand that I will be able to do part of it part of the time, but I just don't think I will be able to do all of it all of the time. The beauty is that it is not only up to me. I know a secret—if you look at the men and women in the Bible who were loved by God because of their faith, you will see that they, like us, didn't have it all together.

Let's take another look a Noah. Who was he? Aside

from being the guy who built a crazy giant boat in the middle of the desert just because God said so, he was just a guy. And he was not perfect. Although the Bible said God chose Noah because he walked with God, it never said he was perfect. I am quite sure that there were days when he was depressed, angry, confused, and frustrated.

He was human. In fact, he was so human that after God made the rainbow covenant with him, he got drunk. There was a little time between the covenant and the party because Noah grew the grapes and made the wine. However, he was drunk enough that he was lying naked in his tent. The story tells us that Noah's youngest son, Ham, saw him naked and, instead of covering him, went off and told his brothers. The two brothers, Shem and Japheth, were concerned for their father's reputation and threw a blanket over Noah. When Noah woke from his bender, he cursed Ham and blessed the other two. So much for starting humanity over without a lot of drama.

We can only assume that Noah lived out the remainder of his nine-hundred-and-fifty years with nothing else going on. I like to think that he continued to walk with God up to his death. We aren't told what he did. What I do know is that his relationship with God is what saved him and his family from destruction.

Moses is another person who God met out in the middle of the ordinary. Although he was tending sheep when God got his attention through a burning bush, he was also a murderer with quite a temper. At the burning bush moment, Moses was a man on the run. He was a stuttering introvert, and God plucked him out of his mediocrity and sent him on the greatest reconnaissance mission known to humankind.

He was sent to gather up around six hundred thousand men with their wives and children and lead them out of captivity. Keep in mind that Moses was a wanted man in Egypt; he had run in fear of being punished by Egypt for forty years. God sent him into his greatest fear to get the "multitude of Israelites," and Moses went. I know that Moses argued with God. I know that God provided a helper for him. I know that Moses was fearful and hesitant. I also know that he went. No matter what else happened, Moses did what he was asked to do. He was just a man, and before this point, we don't know that he spent any time with God. His father-in-law was a Midianite priest. The Midianites worshipped a multitude of gods. That being said, from the moment God spoke to Moses, Moses pretty much dropped everything and followed. So what about Moses's temper? God asked him to touch a rock with his rod to produce water, and Moses hit the rock out of frustration. That is the act that kept Moses from entering the promised land.

What else do we know? We know that, regardless of what he was feeling or going through, he believed what God told him and did what God said. Remember when the Israelites were being bit by poisonous serpents? God told Moses to create a bronze snake and place it on a stick so that whoever looked at it and believed would be healed. I am sure many of the Israelites thought he had lost his mind because, while they were dying, he was in his tent making a bronze snake. He was not deterred by how crazy this looked, and those who believed him and looked upon the snake were healed. I can't find where Moses is described as anything more than a man who, for the most part, followed God. While he wasn't perfect, once he answered the call, he submitted to being in a relationship with God. God seeks out men like Noah and Moses who want to walk with him.

What about Abraham? Abraham, the father of the Jewish nation, was a known liar. Just look at some of his dealings. During his life, he demonstrated impressive acts of faith, and he also failed miserably.

Although Abraham tried to walk with God, he was at times led by impatience or fear instead of God. Let's not forget that, out of fear of being killed, Abraham told his wife Sarah to pretend to be his sister. He did this not once but two different times. Both resulted in Sarah's being taken as a potential wife for another man.

Both times, God intervened to keep her from being with a person other than Abraham. But still, God made a covenant with this man, and even though Abraham failed repeatedly, God never failed him. By the time God asked Abraham to sacrifice his son, he didn't even flinch.

He had come a long way. He had taken great strides to become the man God saw him as being. All of the growth and change was a result of his relationship with God. Through that relationship, regardless of Abraham's successes and despite his failures, God stayed with him and, in the end, Abraham is still known as a man of great faith.

Let's jump forward to King David, the man after God's own heart. You know David—he was the shepherd who was anointed to become the next king. He was the one man brave enough to face Goliath. He was also sometimes arrogant, an adulterer, a murderer, and a schemer. He was not always a good man, but he was known as a man after God's heart. It doesn't make sense. You would think that God would look for good men to work through, men who could keep the commandments. But these are not the people with whom God chooses to work. Although David had some fantastic times of faithfulness, his life was also marked by his failures. Think of Bathsheba and David. The story about them is that David had stayed home from war, and one evening he just happened to be surveying his kingdom from his palace roof and saw her bathing. She must have been pretty hot because David inquired about her. He found out that she was the wife of Uriah, one of his soldiers who was out fighting the war.

That didn't seem to matter to David; he sent for her and slept with her. She became pregnant. David, thinking he could cover up the whole mess, called Uriah away from the battle to spend the night at home. Let's just say it did not work out, so, long story short, David sent Uriah to the front lines of the fiercest battle, where he was killed. If this story sounds too fantastic, you may read it in 2 Samuel 11:1–17. David's relationship with Bathsheba resulted in times of sorrow and heartbreak.

Always, when in the middle of his sorrow, David called out to God. You may be interested to know that David is the author of seventy-three of the one hundred and fifty psalms, including the Twenty-Third Psalm:

> The LORD is my shepherd;
> I shall not want.
> He makes me lie down in green pastures;
> He leads me beside the still waters.
> He restores my soul;
> He leads me in the paths of righteousness
> For His name's sake.

Yea, though I walk through the valley of the
shadow of death,
I will fear no evil;
For You are with me;
Your rod and Your staff, they comfort me.
You prepare a table before me in the presence
of my enemies;
You anoint my head with oil;
My cup runs over.
Surely goodness and mercy shall follow me
All the days of my life;
And I will dwell in the house of the LORD
Forever. (Psalm 23:1–6)

This psalm sure sounds like it was written by someone who, despite all of his failures, lived in relationship with the Lord. Again, we see that a relationship with the Lord is the key to faith.

You may be thinking this is all fine and good, but we need some New Testament faith heroes. So let's take a look at James and John, the sons of Zebedee. In Luke 9:54, it is recorded that James and John were frustrated because they, along with Jesus and the other disciples, were unable to get a room in Samaria for the night. In their anger, they asked Jesus if he wanted them to call down fire from heaven and destroy the village. Talk about a need for anger management! Of course, Jesus says no and rebukes them, and they all go to another town. It is no wonder Jesus nicknamed them the sons of thunder.

Along with James and John, Peter traveled with Jesus as one of the disciples. You may be familiar with Peter's greatest known failure. While eating at Passover with Jesus,

Peter declared his allegiance to Jesus. Jesus told him that, before the rooster crowed, Peter would have betrayed him three times. It is heartbreaking to read how, after Jesus was taken and beaten, Peter, each time he was asked, said, "I don't know that man." The Bible says that when he uttered those words the third time, they were punctuated by the crowing of the rooster. He was so devastated that he quit. The next time we read about Peter, he was fishing with other exdisciples.

Think about this. Peter was crushed. His dreams had all evaporated, and his betrayal rang in his ears. His purpose, passion, and friend were all lost. We read about him sitting on a boat, having fished all night but catching nothing. He was a failure at being a disciple, and now he was a failure in his first night back fishing. In the middle of his sea of hopelessness, a voice called out, "Have you caught anything?" He, along with the others on the boat, answered no. Then Jesus said—for the second time to Peter—"Cast your net on the other side of the boat." And for the second time in Peter's life, the fish so filled the nets that he and the others could not pull them in.

I'm not sure if John told Peter that the man calling to them from the shore was Jesus or if Peter realized it on his own. What I do know is that Peter jumped in and swam to shore. What followed was the loving restoration of Peter. Jesus said three times, "Peter, do you love me?" And three times, Peter answered, "Lord, you know I do."

Why did Jesus so lovingly and gently restore Peter? Just days before, Peter had betrayed him and then ran back to his old way of life as if Jesus had never lived. That doesn't matter to the Lord. While Peter isn't perfect, he was in a relationship with Jesus. The relationship depended on

Jesus. Peter would never be able to live the relationship perfectly, but Jesus could and did perfectly restore him when he failed.

While these are just a few examples of how God chose to work with less-than-perfect but genuinely passionate men, there are many more. Sometimes when we read the New Testament, it seems that the disciples, Paul, and others were perfect. This is only because, except for the Gospels and Revelation, the New Testament is composed of a bunch of letters. Very seldom do they address the flaws of the individuals serving. The Old Testament is very different. It sets forth a love story between God and humankind. We see a perfect God setting out to build relationships, make promises, and redeem humanity. We see him working with imperfect people like those we've listed and a host of others.

God chooses to work through women, too, although we don't have complete stories. He worked through Rahab, the prostitute; Mary of Magdala, who had been possessed by demons; Mary and Martha, the sisters of Lazarus who blamed Jesus for the death of their brother; and others.

I have come to understand that God is capable of working with all of us who see ourselves as a hot mess. God does not like sin, but he sure loves that sinner. While doing all of the things listed in this book will strengthen you, they are utterly useless if they are not leading you into a better love relationship with the Lord. It is my prayer that we Christians will wake up and realize that the holy God of the universe is courting us. He is smitten and wants nothing more than for us to return the love to him that he is giving.

If we were equally in love with the Lord, we would see him as the treasure in the field or the perfect pearl and give up everything for him. In Matthew 13:44–46, Jesus likens the pearl and the treasure to the kingdom of heaven. Please know that the kingdom of heaven is wrapped up in a relationship with the Lord. Along with a place to spend eternity in God's presence, the kingdom provided through a relationship with Jesus allows us to spend our present in his presence.

Folks, if the behaviors listed in this book are not the result of a relationship with the Lord, they will become an unbearable burden to carry. Please hear me—the most important thing is to do what Deuteronomy tells us to do: Love the Lord with all your heart, with all your strength, and with all your might.

If you are doing that, the rest will begin to develop in you. You see, a thankful heart is a result of understanding deep down that all you need is the love of Jesus. When you love the Lord and understand what he has provided, you can't help but talk about it. When you take the time to get to know God personally, it is much easier to trust him over yourself. The love of God brings out the authentic person. In God's light, there are no shadows in which to hide. When you trust someone with all of your heart, courage is a byproduct. A relationship with the Lord provides a protective barrier. That time spent in his Word serves as a boundary around your soul that allows only the truth to enter. As Jesus said, "If you love me, keep my commandments." Out of love comes a desire to please the object of our affection, and that desire to please is expressed as obedience. True love knows no bounds. All of the great love stories lead us to believe that if it is true love, it is unrestrained. That is how it should be. Finally, a relationship that is focused on serving the object of desire is always selfless.

While all of the tenacious faith attributes can be worked on, they emerge from a passionate relationship with the Lord. Unfortunately, much of the church has become bored with Christ. The one for whom they once swooned has become uninteresting. This is not okay. A friend once told me that love is not a feeling; it is a commitment. She said she had been married for over thirty years, and during that time, she had experienced passion and love, as well as disinterest and anger. She said that in one particularly dark period, she had even felt disgusted. She went on to say that had she counted on her feelings, she and her husband would have been divorced by year ten. Instead, she relied on her commitment to him. Please know that God's love for you is based on his commitment to you, and he has promised that once you are his, he will never leave you. Let your commitment guide you to allow the Holy Spirit to work in your heart and create in you a tenacious faith.

If you have made it to this point in the book and realize that you do not have a relationship with the Lord, it is not too late. You need to stop everything and ask Jesus to be your Lord and Savior. In that time of commitment, give him your past, present, and future. Let him take your heart of stone and give you a heart of flesh that can truly love him and others. Consider this your time of making a covenant with God. You are now a team; you are not on your own. Now you begin walking on the path of getting to know this God who loves you so.

Many people are afraid that a relationship with God means they will have to give up a lot. When I was in college, my dad gave his life to the Lord, and one of his friends from his wilder days came to the house to talk with him. They spoke of many things, including heaven, hell, and sin. My dad's friend asked, "When you were hanging out with me and the guys, didn't you have fun?" My dad said, "I did. You are my friends, and I would be lying if I said it wasn't fun." The man then, thinking he had my dad in a corner, asked, "Haven't you given up a lot to become a Christian?" My dad smiled and said, "Maybe, but it is nothing in relation to what I have gained. I traded a life full of hangovers, cover-ups, and chaos for a life of clear-mindedness, honesty, and peace. When you trade with God, there is always a high price, but he is the one who pays it. He makes sure that we get to trade up."

Friend, if you already have a love relationship with God, protect it. Even if you are already committed to him, spend time courting him. Take time to love him. Don't just take him your list of needs; take him your heart. The life of a Christian isn't easy, but it is incredible. It allows the insignificant to become important, the common to become exceptional, and the weak to become strong. Through a relationship with Christ, you, too, can have tenacious faith.

SCRIPTURE INDEX

All Scripture is given by inspiration of
God and is profitable for doctrine, for
reproof, for correction, for instruction
in righteousness, that the man of
God may be complete, thoroughly
equipped for every good work.
—2 Timothy 3:16–17

The scripture is categorized by the words from the acrostic:

Thankful
Evangelistic
Nonsubjective
Authentic
Courageous
Impervious
Obedient
Unrestrained
Selfless

Scriptures on Being Thankful

Ezra 3:11
Psalm 7:17
Psalm 35:18
Psalm 69:30
Psalm 95:1-3
Psalm 100:4-5
Psalm 106:1
Psalm 107:21-22
Psalm 118:1
Psalm 147:7

Daniel 2:23
Habakkuk 3:15-19
Ephesians 5:18-20
Philippians 4:6-7
Colossians 2:6-7
Colossians 3:15-17
Colossians 4:2
Thessalonians 5:16-18
Hebrews 12:28-29
Hebrews 13:15-16

Scriptures on Being Evangelistic

Psalm 105:1
Isaiah 12:4
Matthew 5:14
Matthew 5:15-16
Matthew 28:19-20
Mark 16:15
John 20:21
Acts 1:8
Acts 13:47

Acts 20:24
Romans 1:16
Romans 10:17
1 Corinthians 2:2
1 Corinthians 3:9
1 Corinthians 15:1-2
2 Thessalonians 2:14
2 Timothy 4:2
1 Peter 3:15

Scriptures on Being Nonsubjunctive

Proverbs 3:5
Proverbs 18:12
Proverbs 28:26

Hosea 10:13
Romans 7:5
James 1:8

Scriptures on Being Authentic

Psalm 73:1
Matthew 5:8
James 2:18-26
Romans 12:9
2 Corinthians 1:12

Romans 12:2
Ephesians 4:15

Scriptures on Being Courageous

1 Chronicles 28:20
1 Corinthians 15:58
Deuteronomy 31:6-8
Ephesians 6:10
Isaiah 54:4
John 14:27
Psalm 27:1
Psalm 56:3-4

2 Timothy 1:7
Joshua 1:9-11
Isaiah 41:10-13
1 Corinthians 16:13
Psalm 27:14
Psalm 112:7
Joshua 1:6
Psalm 31:24

Scriptures on Being Impervious

Psalm 1:1-3
Proverbs 1:10-15
John 15:19
Acts 2:40
Romans 12:2
Galatians 6:14

Ephesians 5:11
2 Thessalonians 3:6
2 Timothy 2:4
Hebrews 11:24-25
1 John 2:15

Scriptures on Being Obedient

Deuteronomy 5:33
Deuteronomy 8:6
Deuteronomy 10:12
Deuteronomy 11:22
Deuteronomy 19:9
Deuteronomy 26:17
Deuteronomy 28:9
Deuteronomy 30:16
Joshua 22:5
1 Kings 2:3

1 Kings 3:14
1 Kings 8:58
1 Kings 11:38
Psalm 128:1
Jeremiah 7:23
Zechariah 3:7
Luke 23:56
Romans 6:16
2 Corinthians 9:13
2 Corinthians 10:6

Scriptures on Being Unrestrained

1 Samuel 12:24
Psalm 96:1
Romans 12:1

Romans 14:6
1 Corinthins 10:31
1 Peter 4:2

Scriptures on Being Selfless

1 Corinthians 10:24
1 Peter 3:8
1 Thessalonians 5:15
James 3:16

Mark 12:31
Philippians 2:3
Philippians 2:4
Romans 12:1–2